The Finished Kingdom

A STUDY OF THE ABSOLUTE

Other Writings by Lillian DeWaters

All Things Are Yours ◆ The Atomic Age
The Christ Within ◆ Gems
God Is All and Selected Writings
The Great Answer ◆ Greater Works
I Am That I Am ◆ In His Name
The Kingdom Within
Light of the Eternal
Loving Your Problem ◆ The Narrow Way
The One ◆ Our Sufficient Guide
Practical Demonstration ◆ The Price of Glory
Private Lessons ◆ Science of Ascension
The Seamless Robe & Our Victory
The Time Is at Hand ◆ The Voice of Revelation
Who Am I◆ The Word Made Flesh

The Finished Kingdom

A STUDY OF THE ABSOLUTE

Lillian DeWaters

The Finished Kingdom

Mystics of the World First Edition 2018
Published by Mystics of the World, Eliot, Maine
ISBN-13: 9781946362223
ISBN-10: 1946362220

Cover graphics by Mary Pat Mahan
Printed by CreateSpace
Available from Mystics of the World and Amazon.com

ல் ஆ

DeWaters, Lillian, 1883–1964
The Finished Kingdom originally published by:
Lillian DeWaters Publications
Stamford, Connecticut 1925

Contents

He who illuminates his mind with recognition and contemplation of heavenly things has entered a new order. He who places the inner eye toward the finished kingdom has entered a new freedom.

—Lillian DeWaters

PREFACE

Those who have found help in my early writings and those who have gained additional inspiration from my later writings will, of one accord, report a greater help and fuller understanding in *The Finished kingdom*, which opens up a still higher realm—the realm of the super kingdom.

In this book is presented the Science of Reality, the Science of the Absolute. It lifts one into the realm of intuition, inspiration, illumination, faith—the realm of the fourth dimension, or cosmic Consciousness. This book presents a quality of consciousness that transcends thought, a something that precedes thought and directs thought.

Many are practicing a method of healing that is psychological, believing that it is a spiritual method of healing and that it is the highest way. "There is nothing good or bad, but thinking makes it so" is the edict of the mental plane, but the finished kingdom, the plane of the Absolute and the plane of the fourth dimension of Life, transcends even this law and shows forth a new law of a still higher order: "Behold, I make all things new."

It is well to know that there is a plane of Life higher than the mental plane; that the Science of the Absolute discloses the Christ of God and makes plain a realm wherein healing and deliverance are instantaneous and at hand.

The true teacher is ever himself ascending into higher revealments and is found opening up the way for others. There is no living teacher, however, now demonstrably great enough to be considered final authority on Truth. As the real Self wakens, It neither binds others, nor will It allow Itself to be in bondage to thoughts, reasons, edicts, or credentials. Its view is upward by high watch to high God! Its foundation is the impersonal Truth!

"Make thine own way; and, if thou strayest, listen for the mountain horn, and it will call thee back to the path that goeth upward" (Mary Baker Eddy).

Truth is exhaustless, and as the demand for more Truth is felt in the hearts of men, thus will Truth more clearly make Itself known on earth as it is in heaven.

High Truth carries beauty and message wholly Its own and is altogether impersonal. The quotations from other authors that I have made in this book are not made to make clearer the meaning of these authors or to substantiate anything that I myself set forth. I have merely quoted sentences that give forth the same message that I am giving—roses from the same garden.

Truth forever stands alone, peerless. Truth that is proclaimed by anyone *was* before he proclaimed it and *will be* throughout all eternity. Thus is Truth impersonal, triumphant, and eternal.

Truth spiritually presented heals the sick and the sinner today as it did centuries ago, and those who have eyes to see and ears to hear will find in these pages health and salvation, living water and heavenly bread.

Truth as set forth in this book is not new; rather is it old—old as the Ancient of Days.

—The Author

Word of Life, most pure, most strong!
Lo! for thee the nations long;
Spread, till from its dreary night
All the world awakes to light!
—J. Bahnmaier

Man is the power of the Word. Man is the proof of the omnipotence, omniscience, and omnipresence of God. This is why he can demonstrate "all sufficiency in all things."

—Lillian DeWaters
Practical Demonstration

Chapter I

PREACH THE GOSPEL

The question that has always been deepest in the heart is "What is Truth?" We know that as we unfold in understanding, the Truth that we see and feel today may become even plainer, nearer and dearer to us tomorrow or next month or next year. The path of disclosure is infinite. It has *no* end. Why? Because God is the light thereof.

Truth is not something that is made, set aside, or created by thought or feeling. Truth is *above* all thought and all feeling. Truth is that which *is*. That which is undefilable, that which is indestructible, that which is unspoilable is Truth! That which is immaculate, glorious, and triumphant is Truth! While there are those who are looking to books for Truth, looking to the voices of the living-dead for Truth, still and above all is the silent cry of the living Christ: "I am the Truth."

We gain much from certain books, much from certain teachers, but the greatest gain of all comes to us as we find Truth within ourselves and say understandingly, with the peerless Teacher, "I am the Truth." The world is flooded with metaphysical books. Some teach Truth in this way, others in *this* way, and hundreds are the ways of presenting what seems to the mind of the writer to be Truth. Many write to their teachers asking, "What do you think of this book?" Or, "Is that a good book for me to read?" There is a key that unlocks this mystery concerning books. With this key in our possession, we can read any book on earth and *decide for ourselves* whether

11

or not it is the teaching we desire to practice or the book we ought to study.

As there is what is called a physical plane, also a mental plane of life, so is there a super-mental plane of life. Broadly speaking, we find that there are three planes, or realms, of consciousness.

The lowest plane of life is called the material. Yet, in reality, there is nothing material in the universe. The dictionary tells us that the word *matter* means "something separate or apart from mind." Now, there is really no inanimate thing in the universe that did not spring from mind or thought; hence, all things, whether good or bad, are really not material things, but are mental things. However, the plane is called material, and it is the plane of *things.*

On this plane, things hurt; the weather causes sickness; certain drugs are health-giving, certain drugs are poisonous. There are good things and there are bad things, and the *thing* has the power—that is, the power seems to be in the thing itself. As it is an objective plane, there is found an objective God to govern and control.

Certain laws are found to govern this plane. For instance, if one swallows a poison, he may die; if one is exposed to rain or wind, he may become sick; if one comes in contact with what is called contagious disease, he may take upon himself the same. The thing that is called disease is cured by another thing that is called medicine. This plane is called material because those on this plane have not yet wakened to the power of thought, and they believe that a thing is separate from the thought; thus, the healing on this plane is called material or physical healing.

The second plane is called the mental plane, for this is the plane of thought. Things are not called material on this plane, but all things are found to be mental, proceeding from the mind or thought. Thus, thought is the power that rules this plane. Here it is not the disease that hurts and kills, but it is the *belief* or *thought* about the disease that harms. It is not the weather that brings a cold, but it is the belief in it which is injurious, that causes the trouble. It is not the thing but the *fear of* the thing that is evil. We find here good thoughts and bad or erring thoughts, and the good thoughts are used to overcome the erring thoughts or beliefs. The ruling power, or God, of this plane is right thought.

We find certain cosmic laws governing this plane, the most important being "as a man thinketh in his heart, so is he." This is the law of the mental plane only. This means: think good and you will reap good; think evil and you will reap evil. On this plane of action, *things* have advanced to *thoughts*, and the individual mentality is the seat of individual power. This is the realm of reason, the realm of mental law, and the healing is called mental healing or "right thought" healing.

Now, there is a science that transcends both the so-called material and mental sciences—a science that is *above* both. This science is the divine Science, the spiritual science; the science of reality; the science of perfection; the science of *Isness*. It is the plane of the heavenly law; the plane of ministering angels; the plane of the Holy Ghost; the plane of the Perfect Land; the plane of the new Jerusalem. It is the plane of the fourth dimension; the plane of truth; the plane of the risen Christ. It is the plane of the *finished kingdom.*

The only God recognized on this plane is the I AM. The healing produced by means of this science is called spiritual healing, or divine healing. The law governing this plane is the law of harmony without interruption, limitation, time, or place.

As there are certain laws governing each science and each plane of procedure, so is there a distinct language used on each plane. The plane of the so-called material has a name for every ill feeling of every nature and every kind; a name for each separate sin and a name for millions of drugs and healing means and lotions. The name for the God of this plane is "the Lord."

On the mental plane are also certain words and a different language used. We hear such words as *belief, error, good, harmonious, supposition; mental conviction,* etc. The God of this plane is "Mind."

On the plane of the highest, we speak in "new tongues," a mysterious language to all except those speaking from this height. We hear the words *faith, inspiration, intuition, vision, heavenly law.* As this is the supernal plane, we find no name for what is called, on the lower planes, evil. Tears have been washed away; broken hearts have been bound up; sins have been forgiven. The name of the God on this plane is "the Self-existent," "the Sustaining Infinite," "the I Am."

Now, pick up any book on the subject of life from any plane and test it by this key: is the author writing from the plane of things, the so-called material plane? Is the author writing from the plane of thought, the mental plane, the science of right thinking? Or is the author writing from the high plane, the science of unchanging reality, the plane of the finished kingdom?

After determining for yourself the plane upon which the book at hand is written, you are then in a position to decide and know for yourself whether that book is the book you ought to study. You need not ask any authority. You yourself know whether you prefer the so-called physical, the mental, or the supernal Science. If you will use this key, you will always be able to be your own judge; you will need the advice of no one. *From what plane of*

Life is this book written? This is the question that is the key to the mystery of books.

Spiritual perception must ever accompany the letter, else the letter killeth. Spiritual perception is the love, the feeling, the vision, the Christ-Consciousness expressed by the author in his book and is felt by the reader as he is reading it.

It may not yet have been discovered by many who read these lines that as we proceed toward higher planes we discern a difference between mental healing and the healing that comes from recognition of the finished kingdom. Mental healing is the application of the power of the individual mentality through right thought convictions. Recognition of the finished kingdom takes us into the realm of inspiration, illumination, and wakes the consciousness that *there is nothing to heal.*

Much of the metaphysical teaching of today strives to make plain a way in which health and wealth and happiness are to be worked into manifestation. Mental science teaches the power of the individual mind or thought and the way in which right thought may be directed to heal wrong thought. The right use of the power of the mind is a wonderful step to take, but there is still a higher way for those who are willing to accept it.

There is certainly no condemnation of the lesser methods, but it should be known that the ability to produce health, wealth, fame, and name after this manner will not completely satisfy, nor is it the ultimate Way. Spiritual freedom, heavenly harmony, is won only by recognition of the highest.

The method of thinking that you are getting better day by day is indeed helpful to those who are reaching up to the mental plane. Let us see to it that we are progressing, advancing, always on and up. This book takes you beyond metaphysics, the study of the mentality and its use and power, and reveals to you the spiritual realm—the realm of intuition, love, faith, inspiration, illumination, vision—and points out that state of consciousness wherein healing is spontaneous and wherein "all things shall be added."

This plane has been called the spiritual or mystical plane because it is *above* reason. Reason can only comprehend the things and thoughts that it can see and handle. While right reason is the door to the mental plane, it is not the door to the finished kingdom. Faith is the door, and faith is ever a mystery to reason.

The Master said to his students, "Unto you it is given to know the mystery of the kingdom," and Paul said, "We speak the wisdom of God in a mystery."

A miracle is a marvel. It shows forth the way of the finished kingdom. As one ascends in vision, he beholds the light, and the mystery disappears.

The greatest leader lived and taught from the high spiritual realm. He did not need to heal disease, either by certain things or by certain thoughts. He brought light to the consciousness of the sick, and as light removes darkness by its own presence, so the sick were healed.

Believe that ye *have,* and ye shall manifest. "Look unto me and be ye healed, all the ends of the earth," resounds the voice of the great I AM.

Listen to the covenant from this Source:

> I am the almighty God … I AM THAT I AM … Do not I fill heaven and earth? Before me there was no God formed, neither shall there be after me. Behold, I am the Lord, the God of all flesh … the same yesterday, today, and forever … I am the first, and I am the last; and beside me there is no God … Yea, before the day was, I am he … Is there a God beside me? Ask what ye will. Before they call, I will answer, and while they are yet speaking, I will hear.

16

No weapon that is formed against thee shall prosper ... Fear not the reproach of men ... nothing shall hurt you. Behold, I give unto you power to tread on serpents ... I give life to the faint ... When thou passest through the waters, I will be with thee ... the waters shall not overflow thee ... the fire shall not burn thee.

I will make darkness light before thee ... I will make a way in the wilderness ... I will deliver thee ... I will guide thee ... I will instruct and teach thee ... I will strengthen thee. I will not leave thee nor forsake thee. I will heal thee ... I will take sickness away from the midst of thee.

Eye hath not seen, nor ear heard, the things I have prepared for them that love me ... I give unto him that is athirst of the water of life freely ... I will put a new spirit within you, and make you a new heart.

Call upon me, and I will answer, and will show thee great and mighty things that thou knowest not ... Behold, I make all things new.

Light your mind with high vision, for "where there is no (high) vision, the people perish" (Prov. 29:18).

I now want to call attention to something that *precedes* thought, for there is a something that gives direction to thought and a something that thought follows. It is *vision*. Light your mind with a vision. Look to yourself now and discover for yourself where your vision is. Is your vision directed toward books, toward right thoughts, toward self? Or is your vision toward "the most High"?

Where our vision is, there will our thoughts and feelings be also. We behold a certain goal before us, or we set a certain ideal before us, and then our thoughts and feelings circle around this ideal or vision. "That thou seest, man, that become too thou must" (Brother Angelus). Vision is a looking toward, an inner attention. Thus, we must vision toward the heights if we would ascend thereto. We must keep our vision toward that which is the origin of health, that which is the origin of

17

peace, that which is the origin of victory. The Master said we could not by thought change even our stature. No, not by thought alone. It takes more than thought; it takes right vision.

We often have heard it declared, "I have applied right thought as a healing means, yet I am not receiving healing results." Say a thing once with high recognition! This is more effective than hours of toilsome utterances of simple statements or high statements. Let us not sit still and think a thought over a dozen times or a thousand times like automata. Right instruction can come to us. This, then, is inspiration.

In what direction is our *inner* eye pointed? Is it to the visible or to the Invisible? Is it to the perishable or to the Imperishable? Is it to things and thoughts, or is it fixed to that which is *above* both things and thoughts? We are greater than our thoughts. Let us not make thought our master. We lived and moved and breathed before we ever entertained a single thought. The thinker precedes his thought, and the thinker is greater than his thought.

Truth *is*. We do not have to make Truth. Truth has already made us. Truth is independent of all that we can think or feel or reason. It is our recognition of Truth that *is* that brings us freedom.

There cannot be that which is not. Truth is reality and is all there *is*, the same forever and forever. Truth is perfection, harmony, omnipotence, love. Truth is omnipresent at all times; for as the sky may be hidden by the clouds, so back of all appearances lies reality. Nothing can be added to nor can anything be taken from that which is Truth, nor can It ever be other than Itself. It is original, first, Self-existent, infinite, unbounded, and unlimited. There is no time, no birth, no death, no space, no place, no limitation to Truth that *is.*

The greatest teacher taught and healed up to the time of his resurrection. Preaching and healing go hand in hand. As teachers, we should not teach without practicing our teaching; nor should we heal without enlightening the mind of the patient and pointing the true way to him.

No one can do better than to follow in the footsteps of the Teacher Excelsior. Why should we stop the healing practice until we have arrived at that point of progress where we can "speak the word" and the deaf will hear, the blind will see, and the lame will walk? Let this high goal ever be before us, stirring us into greater endeavor and accomplishments.

One teacher who stands for the Absolute says:

> Muscles highly trained have won out against natural muscles, and thoughts highly practiced have wrought mental havoc. What shall we, who wish to be free and not to engage in warfare, do when our peace and safety are menaced by foes of such giant physical and mental stature? We will seek unto God, the High Presence in the universe not affected by thoughts …
>
> It shall not profit a man to gain the whole world by the prowess of his arm or the might of his thought. It shall only profit him to know his own Soul, uncontaminated offspring of Eternal Majesty, whose triumphs are already complete, ready to manifest …
>
> Let mind no longer claim creative powers or accomplishing energies. The true work is already complete in Spirit, the Self that we praise … We praise the great, free Spirit that stands back of our mind … We praise the free Spirit that knows beyond the mind, which is saying ever, "I am God; I am Truth; I am Light."
>
> —Emma Curtis Hopkins

You will recall that Paul asked the Ephesians, "Have ye received the Holy Ghost since ye believed?" And the reply was, "We have not so much as heard whether there be any Holy Ghost." Those living on the lower planes of life may not yet have heard that there is a supernal kingdom, a divine Science. Divine Science is the science of the Absolute, the science of the finished kingdom. It pertains to that which is back of thought and beyond thought. It pertains to individual Soul, Its illuminations and inspirations and Its unity with I AM THAT I AM.

On the first plane of life, we may be in bondage to things, while on the second plane, one may be in bondage to thoughts. If we are depending entirely upon our right thoughts to deliver us, then if we are so fearful or so ill that we cannot formulate a right thought, are we not hopeless?

The I AM is higher and greater than all thoughts conceivable. To have right thought is right and good, but to worship right thought or to consider it God is not the way of the finished kingdom. "Thou shalt have no other gods before me"—the I AM. Right thought is but the path in which we walk from earth to heaven, from sense to Soul. Loving, truthful, healing thoughts are the wings with which we fly upward and onward.

Our right or wrong viewpoint does not change in any way the viewpoint of the Perfect and the viewpoint of perfect manifestation in the Life element Itself. Our viewpoint merely affects our own individual progress and manifestation. You and I behold a thing or a condition according to our present individual state of perception and understanding. What is meat to one may be poison to another. While the quality in all consciousness remains the same, the quantity varies according to the individual progress or evolution.

Life cannot be life today and death tomorrow; good cannot have been good yesterday and evil today; nor can health be here one moment and gone the next. We must fix our vision on the *Isness* state of Life—the omnipresence of changeless harmony, our infinite divinity. Since the Divine cannot change Its inherent qualities, neither can these inherent qualities of health, activity, strength, courage, love be changed in us.

Does the air ask for invisibility? Do the stars desire to shine? No. Neither do we need to long for that quality which we already inherently possess; thus, we *are* courage, we *are* strength, we *are* power, we *have* abundance. Let man become conscious of what he is! Let him know himself—his inner Self, the Christ-Self—to be all that he could possibly desire! Life gives us earth and heaven, time and eternity, in which to understand this Self, this pearl of great price.

The value of right thought is this:

> Think the thought that harmonizes with the universal fact of life. Then we automatically receive the blessing.

We must think and act according to our highest vision. We must turn our gaze from sorrow and look toward the finished kingdom of triumphant joy; turn our gaze from dying and look toward the finished kingdom of Life everlasting; turn our gaze from sickness and look toward the origin of unspoilable health.

Where was the vision of Jesus when he stood at the grave of Lazarus? Did he, like the rest, look down into the pit to behold a dead, decomposed Lazarus? No. While hundreds around him were thus visioning and weeping, he was sighting the begotten of God, the offspring of I AM THAT I AM. He beheld life that is everlasting, omnipresent, omnipotent, and unspoilable. It was this vision of victorious Life that transcended him.

Where was the vision of Jesus when he stepped out upon the surface of the deep sea? Was it downward into the limpid depths of the ocean, or was it *up,* fastened upon the miracle-working Unseen, transcending the drowning powers of the deep? The eye should be moved from appearances to see the fields already white to harvest, to hear the words of our Redeemer: "Thou art whole!"

Vision toward the plane of ever-present Reality! Time is not a factor here. As we experience illumined consciousness, beholding the ever-present finished kingdom and ourself free Spirit, birthless, deathless, diseaseless, painless, triumphant, and victorious, we find that we are all that we would become.

In order to do the things of Spirit, there must be Soul-enwisdoming, a spiritual recognition or realization of Truth. It is not enough to become aware of the reality of the individual soul; there must also be a consciousness of identity with the universal Life, even as the Master, Jesus, taught and illustrated.

We are Soul-drops in the great ocean of Life. We arc divine sparks of the infinite Light. Taking this as a starting point in the spiritual recognition of our oneness with the Whole, it blesses and enriches us. Each is an individual center of consciousness in the great ocean of Consciousness. How could we then expect to control our thoughts if we do not start on this right foundation—that we are greater than our thoughts? Only as we realize the Self that is *above* thinking do we become capable of controlling our thinking.

Our progress upon Earth does not depend upon the destruction of the body or the destruction of the mind, but absolute Science teaches us the right use of the mind and the right use of the body. The *I* does not depend upon Its thought creation, but the thought creation depends upon the *I*. Even so, mind does not depend upon body, but body depends upon mind.

High consciousness tells us *I am*, and this is the final analysis or conclusion. The I AM is Self-existent.

The mind should obey the *I*; thus are we the master of mind and not its slave or servant. All the sick thoughts

or fear thoughts you have ever thought have never hurt
or harmed the *you* that is Spirit. Water cannot drown it
nor flame burn it nor death kill it, for It is imperishable,
undefilable, indestructible, and immortal. One writer says:

> The *I* is eternal. It passes unharmed through the
> fire, the air, the water. Sword and spear cannot kill
> or wound it. It cannot die ... Blessed is he who can
> say (understandingly) "*I*."

Nothing should daunt or falter the seeking heart, pressing forward toward the high goal, knowing it must forever live and will forever reveal its perfect Self—Christ,
the Head of the house.

> Thus is Christ the head of you and the head of
> your house ... I live, yet not I, but Christ liveth in
> me ... where there is neither Greek nor Jew, bond
> nor free, but Christ is all, and in all ... Therefore, if
> any man be in Christ, he is a new creature ... The
> head of every man is Christ.
>
> —Paul

Render unto each plane the things that belong to
that plane; and render unto the Absolute the things that
belong to the Absolute! Give to the so-called physical
its hospitals, operating rooms, prisons, and graveyards.
Give to the mental realm its high thoughts, right declarations and affirmations. But give to the Absolute Its plane
of unlimited dimensions, miracles, and ministering angels!

As a house has many rooms, and one may sit in the
kitchen or in the parlor, so this universe has invisible
plane upon plane, and one has the divine and cosmic right
to live, move, and breathe in any plane he so decides.
This is our divine birthright—choice.

It is necessary that we rise from ideal to ideal, from
realm to realm, and from "out of the depths" to high deliverance. If the books we read contain uplifting, inspira-

tional, instructive words and ideas ever pointing us to something higher than we as yet have perceived, we read them carefully, to drain from them that vital life that is in them. We should let Spirit be our teacher. As the divine spark that we are gradually comes forth in its own radiance, we are guided aright to higher and still higher heights.

As the mind can enjoy the right pleasures of life and respond in joy to them, so can Soul thrill with heavenly visions and feel the joy-giving touch of divine Presence. Thus the spiritually minded feel a contact, a soul response, from the reading of certain books. Let this inner response, this silent touch, be the guide, the answer, as to the nature and quality of the book we are reading. If, as we read a book, we feel happier and freer, fear thoughts and wrong ideas drop away from us like dead leaves, we rejoice because we are entering a new order of life, and if we continue to look upward, we learn to say fearlessly and triumphantly, "It is" to the true.

We must set ourselves a high vision and hold fast thereto. The mind which follows the rambling senses makes one as helpless as the boat the wind leads astray upon the waters. If we learn something today and yet tomorrow it becomes more clearly known to us, leading us to higher ideals, this is no reason for tears, as if we should say, "How do I know that this also may not alter one way or the other?"

"I will not leave you desolate, but in the Christ, which is the love of God made manifest to man, will I be with you all the way," says the ever-present, impersonal Truth.

This universe of God is far more wonderful than has yet reached the heart of men. "Eye hath not seen, nor ear heard, neither have entered into the heart of man, the things which God hath prepared for them that love him" (1 Cor.

2:9). For instance, we step out into our garden and pick beautiful roses. We watch the birds fly to and fro over our heads and hear them singing at our windows. We play with the sand or marvel at the stars. But who of us enjoys the *unseen* verities? How many of us see the unseen, hear the silence, and feel the touch of light and glory?

We have been taught that in order to have a thought, we must think it. Not so. It is possible to gather a thought out of the invisible element the same as we pluck the visible flower. We can see a flower; why not see a thought? We can hear the musical sound of the Victrola; why not hear the music of the spheres? We can see the light of the sun; why not see the light that transcends the sun?

Oh, it is something to vision toward and delight in, to live in a world where beautiful thoughts float about us, created by the same Source that created us, and where we gather unto ourselves these thoughts the same as we arrest the flight of birds flying near us. And these thoughts are so much more wonderful and so different from any thoughts that are consciously formulated!

Where did the manna come from that the children of Israel found on the ground every morning and which fed them for forty years? Did it grow out of the earth? Oh, no, it was *above*, and they saw it.

Where did the bread come from, and the fish with which Jesus fed nine thousand hungry mouths? Did the bread come from the seeds that were put into the earth, or were the fish gathered from the seas? No indeed. They were present in the great Universal. Jesus saw them *already prepared,* and his vision extended so that they around him saw the same and ate the bread and the fish.

Are we not walking through a *finished* kingdom? Is not heaven *at hand?* Is not the kingdom *without us* as *within us?*

Who was it speaking the words, "This is my beloved Son, in whom I am well pleased"? Was it the voice of any of the people surrounding Jesus at the Jordan? No, they did not speak it, but they heard it. Did Jesus himself say the words with his own lips, so that the multitude heard and saw? No, Jesus himself was listening, not speaking. Did you ever stop to think, or has it ever unfolded to you, that the Universal has voice—that voice, sound, and words can proceed from the depths of the Infinite as well as from the throat of the individual?

Who was the fourth man that was seen walking with the three Hebrew captives in the burning furnace? Did Nebuchadnezzar imagine he saw a fourth? Was the fourth a product of his own imagination? Was not the fourth "like unto the Son of God"? Indeed, the infinite Intelligence in which we live can manifest Itself as form, as well as thought or voice, for those who *believe.*

To whom or to what was Jesus addressing himself when he spoke, "Rather, I thank thee that thou hast heard me"? Was he talking to himself? No, he was recognizing and praising the one Infinite, the All-hearing, the All-knowing, the All-seeing, the All-mighty Omnipresence.

From whence came the angels that shut the lions' mouths for Daniel? That fed Elijah in the wilderness? That stood at the empty sepulchre of Jesus? That revealed the mystery of the kingdom unto John in Patmos?

The great I AM—the All-filling Presence, the All-knowing Reality—can this not make Itself *felt? Seen? Heard? Understood?*

"I am in the Father and the Father is in me." If the Substance that is in you, the Substance that you are, is Intelligence can hear, see, speak, and feel—does not that which is the origin of your substance also have voice, intelligence, understanding?

Blessed are the poor in Spirit, the believing, for they shall see God.

Blessed are they who believe in angels, for they only can behold them.

Blessed are they who listen for the voice of the silence, for they only can hear it.

Blessed are they who look toward unseen thoughts, for they only can gather them.

Blessed are they who believe in miracles, for they only can experience them.

Blessed are they who have faith in the fourth dimension, for they only can enter it.

Blessed are they who vision toward the finished kingdom, for they only can walk in it.

Blessed are they whom the Lord, when he cometh, shall find *watching,* for they only are ready.

In darkness we behold the dark; in the tunnel we see not the light. "I am the door!" exclaimed the great prototype of the finished kingdom. The recognition of the risen Christ is our light out of the darkest tunnel and the blackest night.

Instead of contemplating right reason as the Christ, we now contemplate our real Self as the Christ. Right reason is now but an avenue or means of recognition. Instead of contemplating our right thought as infinite power, we now contemplate the I AM as the one and only Omnipotence within us and above us. Right thought is now but a means, a gift of God, the path from sense to Soul. Instead of contemplating one's individuality as the ultimate recognition, we now contemplate our unity with the Whole, our oneness with the sustaining Infinite.

Instead of consciously directing right thought to heal, we have now risen in consciousness, so that we can "become conscious for a single moment that Life and intelligence are purely spiritual," and when we would manifest divine order, we now:

27

Cling steadfastly to God and His idea. Allow nothing but His likeness to abide in your thought. Let neither fear nor doubt overshadow your clear sense and calm trust, that the recognition of life harmonious—as Life eternally is—can destroy any painful sense of, or belief in, that which life is not ...

Insist vehemently on the great fact that covers the whole ground, that God, Spirit, is all, and that there is none beside Him. There is *no disease* ...

To discern the rhythm of Spirit and to be holy, thought must be purely spiritual ...

Metaphysical healing includes infinitely more than merely to know that mind governs the body and the method of a mental process ... You must first mentally educate (or recognize) the spiritual sense or perceptive faculty by which one learns the metaphysical treatment of disease.

—Mary Baker Eddy

The order, law, and healing on the plane of the great Adequate is not a mystery to Itself or to those whose faces are heavenward; it is only a mystery to those of limited vision and unquickened sense. It is our birthright to dwell in the light ourselves and to point others hitherward. We each have a right to our own light of understanding, and we should look away from all sense of personality to the one high Cause.

When we are thinking in accordance with Truth, this is true thought. When we are in the light, we do not see darkness, and when our sense is illumined by spiritual Truth and vision, we do not see a sick person or a sinner, but like Jesus, we call to the blind man, *See!* knowing that he *can* see.

The drop of water does not lose itself in the big ocean; it simply loses its sense of itself as an independent or separate drop. Nevertheless, it moves on in the allness of the ocean and is part thereof. Thus with us. Knowing that we live, move, and have our being in the infinite I

AM—the omnipresent Omnipotence—we lose sight of any separateness and understand the Master's words, "Thou in me, and I in thee."

The word *miracle* rightly belongs to the high plane of the Absolute. Thus, this plane is called the plane of the miraculous, super logical, or mystical. The *Standard Dictionary* says that a miracle is a wonder possible only by the exertion of divine power and that the supernal or mystical plane is recognized "by direct divine illumination, immediate consciousness, or knowledge of God."

If a person were ill, and under metaphysical treatment recovered gradually so that within a few weeks' time he was again perfectly well, this would not be called a miracle, as would a healing that was *instantaneous.*

In the popular book, *Tertium Organum,* we read the following:

> But what, after all, is mysticism? ... Mystical states of consciousness are closely bound up with knowledge received under conditions of expanded receptivity ...
>
> Until quite recently psychology did not recognize the reality of the mystical experience and regarded all mystical states as *pathological ones* ...
>
> Mystical states give knowledge which nothing else can give. Mystical states give knowledge of the real world with all its signs and characteristics ... The results of the mystical experiences are *entirely illogical* from our ordinary point of view. They are *super-logical.*

All instantaneous healings and deliverances spring from a divine state of consciousness or a spiritualized consciousness. This is the plane or realm of heavenly visions, ministering angels, and mighty things—the plane *above;* the plane wherein Truth *is*; wherein harmony is; wherein is the *finished kingdom.*

It was from this plane that Jesus Christ commanded: See! Hear! Stand up! Walk! Come forth! Arise! It was from this high plane that he cried to the great Invisible yet Ever-present: "Glorify me! Deliver me! Thy kingdom come!"

While it may not be so easy at first for one to follow the law of divine Science, still we should strive to understand it and to demonstrate it. The way of divine Science transcends the mind and its thoughts. Consider these words pertaining to divine Science:

> In divine Science, the universe, including man, is spiritual, harmonious, and eternal ... Divine Science derives its sanction from the Bible, and the divine origin of Science is demonstrated through the holy influence of Truth in healing sickness and sin ...
>
> That those wonders are not more commonly repeated today arises not so much from lack of desire as from lack of spiritual growth ...
>
> Divine Science alone can compass the heights and depths of being and reveal the infinite ... The full Truth is found only in divine Science ... The substance of Truth is discerned only through divine Science ... Heaven is the reign of divine Science.
>
> What but divine Science can interpret man's eternal existence, God's allness, and the scientific indestructibility of the universe? ... One step away from the direct line of divine Science cost them— what? A speedy return under the reign of difficulties, darkness, and unrequited toil.
>
> Christ, God's idea, will eventually rule all nations and peoples—imperatively, absolutely, finally— with divine Science ... So shall all earth's children at last come to acknowledge God, and be one; inhabit His holy hill, the God-crowned summit of divine Science.
>
> —Mary Baker Eddy

There is a state of consciousness above the good and the bad, above the right sense and the wrong sense, above sickness and health, above the high and the low; this state of consciousness is the risen Christ! It is this state of consciousness that sees all as One, and sees one as All, beholding perfection and the finished kingdom now and here!

What we need is this high Truth. Does it make any difference whether we find It in a book or in a newspaper? Does it make any difference whether It is presented to us by a red man or a white man? Does it matter whether Truth is written by one living in the old world or by one living in the new world; whether in Africa or in Alaska? Is there any "thine" or any "mine" to Truth, the flaming Impersonal?

In the early days, great teachers thought it wise to protect their students from spurious reading, feeling, no doubt, that the student himself had not awakened to that perception where he could detect that which *is* from that which is not. This guidance and protection was wise and good and no doubt saved multitudes from byways, keeping their feet in the straight and narrow path. But today there are those of us who have reached the point where we know how to recognize Truth ourselves, and we let every good thought and word aid us heavenward.

In order to recognize the brotherhood of man, we must recognize the Fatherhood of God, and in order to apprehend the Fatherhood of God, we must recognize the brotherhood of man.

A new day, a new order of Life has come. Cosmic Life is moving ever onward. Pick up the feet and stand upon them even more strongly, and continue to watch! To all of us who are earnest, honest, and loving in heart, no lesson ever comes in vain; no lesson ever leaves us where it found us. From out the darkness comes a greater

light than ever before. Let the dead past bury the dead,
but look thou, O Soul, to the risen Christ!

> In all eternity, no tone can be so sweet,
> As where man's heart with God
> In unison doth beat.

—Silesius

The individual may ever feel this unity with the
infinite One.

Humility and meekness precede kingship and authority. Yet whether humble or kingly, it is well to remember
that everyone is of royal birthright and heir to the kingdom.

There is a gate that opens up to celestial glories. It
is seen from the mountain heights, and it is reached after
many experiences in climbing and falling and in climbing
again. Love is the guide, and faith is the star pointing
hitherward. Thought becomes higher and finer only as
it is spiritualized.

"Like a crystal, reflect all light that comes to thee,
and then shall the light of thine own soul become
more and more brilliant."

Now, the world has waited long for a great cosmic religion that should absorb all the truth … It has
also waited for a religion that would appease the
heart hunger of all ages, and also one that would contain within itself a fountain of perpetual inspiration.

To possess this religion in its fullness one must
be able to find the oneness of self with the Infinite
… Love alone hath within itself the power to redeem,
lift up and enlighten the world …

Be as firm and as unyielding in what thou knowest to be right as Truth itself; keep thy whole life
near to the ideal thou hast set up before thee; let love
lead thee ever with her gentle, yet firm, hand along
the pathway that makes for true righteousness …
(then) thou hast found the Perfect Way that leads to
complete mastery of all things.

—G.A.Fuller

To those who may long to reach the way of Spirit yet do not clearly discern It, the Teacher repeats: You can clearly understand that the Thinker must be greater than his thought, that the Manifester must be higher than his manifestation; thus, you are above thoughts of any kind—above trouble, above disease, above death, above the pairs of opposites. The *I* or *Me* of the self is the real Self, the Christ-Self—pure, imperishable Spirit.

As you speak from this Christ-Self, you surely say:

I am Spirit, undefilable, undefeatable, imperishable, impervious, immortal. *I* cannot be touched by trouble of any kind, for *I* am from above. *I* cannot be sick, for *I* am incorruptible. *I* cannot die, for *I* am imperishable. *I* am immaculate, triumphant, original Self!

The realization of one's Self as perfect, divine, and immutable Spirit gives one the power and peace that he needs, and to think, feel, and act from the standpoint of Spirit—the finished kingdom—automatically expands the viewpoint or vision, making room for the ultimate revealment: the Christ and the spiritual body, Soul and Its manifestation, are *one.*

"When the disciple is ready the master is also ready." The Truth we seek is forever within our reach, but each must do his own seeking, the same as each does his own eating and drinking. We can help another to a great extent in making plain the steps which we ourselves have learned through experience, but each one must himself find the Way for himself, and the more illumination and inspiration he possesses the easier the Way becomes.

We came forth from the Infinite, and to the Infinite we go. "I came forth from the Father … and go to the Father."

The baby cannot say, "I am a man," nor can the acorn say, "I am an oak." Yet potentially, the baby is a man and an acorn is an oak. As we gain understanding and demonstrate that understanding by healing the sick, walking on the water, raising the dead, transfiguring ourselves with living glory so that our face "shines as the sun," then we say as did our great Teacher, "He that hath seen me hath seen the Father—I am the life."

The ideal teacher is one who guides us always up and on; points us to the heights and leads us quietly toward them; tells us of the Christ within. Our minds should reach up to this great Truth, as the river seeks the ocean.

Thus it is that on the high plane one does not attempt to make himself well by his formulated thinking, but always and forever he bears uppermost in mind that he is forever well, for that which *is* and that which *shall be* is *now.* We are well now because Truth *is* and we *are,* and we are all that Truth is. If you will light your mind with this high vision, it will lead you to sublime heights.

There is nothing lost, there is nothing sick, there is nothing dead in the finished kingdom of reality. Even a tiny glimpse of this kingdom is quickening and renewing, uplifting and inspiring.

Truth is first. It has no cause. The finished kingdom sets aside the mental law of mental cause and effect. There is nothing to oppose Truth. There is nothing besides Truth. Truth is universal freedom. All things are possible unto us, for we are in and of this Truth. Herein the beginning is as the end, and the end is as the beginning. Herein is permanent *Isness*; herein is changeless Reality; herein is infinite Life and Its infinite, finished wholeness.

Said the Christ, "What I say unto you,
I say unto all, Watch."

Chapter II

HEAL THE SICK

In the Science of God, we look toward the realm of Reality. We describe it, we praise it, we have faith in it, and it manifests unto us. Is not everything already created, already perfect, already changeless, already prepared, already manifested in the finished kingdom? High recognition brings one into the light, and automatically he is lighted.

Light does not have to be acquainted with darkness in order to remove it. Should light search from plane to plane and from eternity to eternity, it would never find darkness, for wherever light might search, it would find only itself, its own radiant brightness.

See the self or the one called patient perfect in the finished kingdom! The real Self is the Christ of God, knowing no sickness, no weakness, or death. Let us refuse to see or to acknowledge any other than this Self. Let us turn our gaze to the kingdom and conform our thoughts thereto, knowing that perfect Life *is* now and forever and that we are now this perfect Life. "Let God be true, but every man a liar" (Rom. 3:4). Let the God-Self, the I AM Self, be the Self that is recognized and understood. Let this Self be true to us and the personal or sick self be the liar.

The Christ knows Itself and knows only Its own brightness, even as light knows itself and knows not darkness, yet removes what is termed darkness by its own presence. We are to see ourself or the patient whole, perfect, complete, harmonious—the living, victorious Christ of the kingdom of God! Do we not read: "And Jesus went about teaching and preaching the gospel of the kingdom ... It is the Father's good pleasure to give you the kingdom ... Behold, the kingdom of God is within you ... Now is come salvation, and strength, and the kingdom of God, and the power of his Christ"?

Not at some future day of disclosure, but *now* the kingdom of heaven *is*. This kingdom is already prepared, already awaiting our claim upon it, our recognition of it, our faith in it, our new birth into it. Though we "walk in the flesh," we should not "war after the flesh," but preach and teach the already prepared kingdom of perfect health and harmony.

"And the nations of them which are saved shall walk in the light of it" (Rev. 21:24). Believing that God's kingdom of perfection is eternally manifested, we begin to find it manifested unto us. This is accomplished by an inner perception, an awareness, a Soul feeling or knowing.

> When you become conscious of a thing, it comes to exist in your mind. Hence, Jesus the Christ said, "The kingdom of God is within you." The mystery of the kingdom is that everything that is eternal in the Divine Plan is also eternal in manifestation. When you realize this mystery, you become free from poverty, misfortune, and all forms of disease.
>
> —*The Mystery of the Kingdom*

The Christ-Self and the kingdom of heaven are already prepared, already waiting our recognition to come forth and transcend our mental life. With expanded vision, we see this manifested kingdom as we walk; we see trees and flowers, brooks and oceans, birds and animals, people and things in a new light. We look upon all of nature's manifestations as the creation of God. Looking upon the grain of sand, we cannot tell how it cometh or whither it goeth, but we know that it is forever held in the bosom of the whole, the same as are the stars in the heavens and the gold in the earth.

It takes spiritual quickening to bring us close to the heart of these divine realities. The more we love, the more we feel, the more Soul illumination and Soul wisdom we experience, the greater is our sense of happiness and our joy in seeing and in associating with all manifestations of Life.

On the mental plane, one finds himself confronted with the idea of time. It takes time to reason, time to think, time to manifest. We reason that while all reality is now in the invisible, all reality is not now manifested to us. This is true reasoning from the mental plane of progress, but in the finished kingdom we eliminate all ideas of within and without; we find the within and without to be one and inseparable, and all to be the *now* and the *here*. We understand that because reality *is*, it is forever manifested!

We now perceive and contemplate the fixed, permanent state of *manifested* harmony. In this kingdom, all ideas are, and all ideas are eternally known. This perception and soul sense that we have of manifested reality and manifested perfection transcends the mental plane, and we see this universe filled with the manifestations of God. "The great spiritual fact must be brought out that man is, not shall be, perfect and immortal."

> Be not afraid, O creatures of the earth!
> The thing you fear is but a senseless cloud.
> In God's name rise! and rend the phantom shroud.
> Lo, o'er the earth Love's presence doth appear;
> The healing Christ triumphant draweth near …
> Arise! and know by Spirit thou wert made
> As perfect as thy God. Be not afraid!
>
> —Willis Cole

Looking toward the finished kingdom, we recognize that all problems have been forever solved, and thus we find the needed solution transcending or breaking forth for us. "Look up; for your redemption draweth nigh."

The understanding of the ever-manifested right ideas and right states is the plane of the miracle—quick healing, quick deliverance. Herein there is nothing to be removed, nothing to be cut out, nothing to be added to or taken from the already finished wholeness. Attention is held fast to the finished work, and we think, act, and feel in this consciousness.

Once, while sitting in a dentist's chair, I glimpsed this great fundamental fact of reality—that in the plane of heaven, no one can be hurt, nor can one hurt another. This was as certain to me as my own being, and at that instant the dentist held his hand poised in the air, grasping a long wire which he was going to thrust into my exposed and waiting gum. For several seconds, through my clear vision of the present facts of the finished kingdom, his extended hand remained poised, still. Then it dropped to his side, and came the awed exclamation, "I cannot do it!"

One might direct conscious thought to another, saying, "You cannot hurt me," or "I, Spirit, cannot be hurt by you," and if one's thought was sufficiently powerful, it would act upon the mind of the other and paralyze his ability to hurt. But the plane of mind over mind or mind over body is not the way of the finished kingdom.

Perfection is not effected by thought of any kind. Perfection belongs to the plane above thought; not a plane where we do not think, but a plane wherein something transcends thought—wherein something gives us a new mind and a new thought.

In the spiritual way, we do not demonstrate over lack, over sickness, over trouble. We demonstrate God! In the experience related above, no thought was directed toward the dentist; no thought was directed toward the condition; no thought was directed toward the self. In the kingdom, there is no power to hurt and no one to be hurt. The consciousness of this eternal, present fact transcended the mental plane and rendered null and void its hurting powers.

The ideal or spiritual method by no means condemns the plane of the mental any more than the plane of the mental condemns the plane of the so-called physical. We are all free beings with given right of choice. Each has the God-given right to think on any plane he chooses. This does not change the fact that the so-called physical man is really mental and that the so-called mental man is really spiritual, or as it has sometimes been expressed— mystical. We can bless the doctors who are giving their lives to help mankind; bless the metaphysicians who are doing their utmost to bring Truth on earth as it is in heaven; bless the churches that are housing the hungry, the weary sinner, and the mourner.

Jesus did not condemn the lower planes; still, he ever pointed to the higher plane. He blessed the bread and meat, yet he pointed to the bread of Life and said, "I have meat to eat that ye know not of." This meat was from *above.*

He blessed right thought and believed in right thinking and feeling, yet he pointed still higher, for he said, "In such an hour as ye think not, the Son of man cometh" That is, while the mind is still from outward or conscious reasoning, the Christ is recognized. "Why take ye thought? Why reason ye?"

He preached in the temples, yet he called attention to perfect worship: "The hour cometh, when ye shall neither in this mountain, nor yet at Jerusalem, worship the father

... when the true worshippers shall worship the Father in spirit and in truth" (John 4:21, 23).

"I am the bread of life! I am the light of the world! I am the resurrection! I am the life! I am the door! I am the truth!" were the ringing declarations from the representative of the finished kingdom. The disciples also recognized this truth, for they cautioned, "Seek those things which are above ... Set your affection on things above ... Every good and every perfect gift is from above."

The science of God is above the range of the reasoning faculty, and mind gladly drops its argumentative methods as it catches glimpses of this heavenly land. There is nothing about which to reason in the realm of *Isness.* Except you become as a little child, you cannot see the kingdom of Spirit is what the Master said. The little child does not reason or seek to prove; it labors not and is carefree.

To sit still and argue "why" and "how" gives no time for the Christ to speak, and while the mind is noisy it does not hear the "still small voice." The Christ of God reasons not. The Christ of God *knows.*

Did not the great Jesus say, "My kingdom is not of this world"? He represented the kingdom of *above*—the Perfect Land.

In the lesser kingdoms, we have sorrow and joy, death and life, weakness and strength, sinners and saints; but in the kingdom of the heavenly law, tears, death, and sickness are unknown. "Lift up your heads ... and the King of glory shall come in," the real King, the Christ divine.

Recently I read a Bible quotation and its inner meaning from the pen of a noted writer, and it opened up a wonderful truth to me. The Bible quotation was this: "Then shall two be in the field; the one shall be taken, and the other left." Previously I had never given this saying of the Master any special attention, but now it rings with a wealth of meaning. We have heard about the mortal and the immortal, the real and the unreal, the outer and the inner, the old and the new man—these are the two.

The Christ-Self, the God-Self, the real Self, is the inner Self—the Self that is immaculate, peerless, imperishable. This Christ-Self ever waits our recognition.

I am reminded of an incident that occurred during the past summer. While standing one day near a tree, I noticed a bug clinging to it. Looking more closely, it appeared to be just a brown beetle with nothing especially peculiar about it, but as I watched it, lo and behold, it came apart, and there in front of my very eyes, the bug that I saw became two bugs. From out the dark brown shell emerged a beautiful green locust.

With attention riveted to this transformation, I took in every detail. The two bugs were now before me attached by a tiny white cord or thread, and for the space of an instant both bugs were alive. The eyes in the brown shell were open, and there also stood the live, sparkling-eyed, green beetle. Then the thread snapped, the eyes of the brown bug closed. 1 picked it up; it was nothing but a dead, empty shell. And there stood the live, green creature in all its new beautiful garment!

From this I learned a deep lesson—the lesson of "two in the field; one is taken and the other left." The question is: which of the two are we claiming to be? Which are we taking and which are we leaving? Are we taking the sick, sinning, unhappy self around with us, leaving entirely out of sight the real Christ-Self, flawlessly perfect and free but unknown to us? Or are we leaving the "I can't" self and taking the Christ-Self as the *only* Self? It was the way-shower himself who said, "There shall be two in the field; one shall be taken and the other left." We cannot serve two masters. Which self are we recognizing? Which self are we acknowledging? Which self are we expressing?

> There are two selves; the higher and lower self … The lower self is an illusion and will pass away, but the higher self is God in man and will never pass away. The lower self is the embodiment of truth reversed, and so falsehood is manifested. The higher self is justice, mercy, love, and right, but the lower self is what the higher self is not.
>
> He who knows his lower self knows the illusions of the world and the things that pass away; he who knows his higher self knows God and knows well the things that cannot pass away.
>
> —*The Aquarian Gospel*

Since God is too pure to behold iniquity, how do we account for these pairs of opposites, right and wrong, sickness and health, good and evil—these "two in the field"?

These pairs have appearance in the lower planes but are unknown in the finished kingdom. There is no law of judgment in the Science of Reality. There is no law to fit thoughts or to fit deeds. "I know 'the law to fit the deed' hath no terrors for him who is shaping his course *above* the law." The law of punishment does not exist in the high plane, for there is nothing to hurt and nothing to be harmed; no one to sin and no one to sin against. Jesus was speaking from this high plane when he asked, "Which one of you convinceth me of sin?"

Herein is the mystery unveiled. To the consciousness beholding the perfect, *there is no sin.*

The true Self is above all erring thoughts or erring conditions. Confidence, peace of mind, faith, understanding establish the right foundation for revealment of the perfect Selfhood. We must look away from appearance toward reality; see it as though it were visibly before us. Such right vision and perception transcends the mind and causes us to declare, "I am whole!"

Spiritual healing is of Spirit, automatically adjusting the thoughts, flooding the mind with the divine light of inspiration, and bringing peace, uplift, joy, and harmony. Salvation is founded upon the rock of Christ; hence, when visioning toward the finished kingdom, we look above the individual mentality with its right thoughts and wrong thoughts; above the "two in the field." We look to the white Christ, the free Spirit forever glorious, forever triumphant, forever manifesting Its perfect Self-hood—the Christ of God!

Called to the home of one who seemed to be passing from this earth, I found the patient had been unconscious for two days; the doctors claimed paralysis of the throat. Entering the sickroom, I took a seat by the window, closed my eyes and my thought entirely to the patient, and turned my gaze to the kingdom of God and the kingdom's perfect manifestation.

The vision was lifted above a closed throat and above an open throat, above thoughts and above things. I looked and beheld Spirit—Self-sustaining—and saw the "water of life" proceeding from Life Itself, which is ever in-drinking and inbreathing its own glorious ideas. "The water that I shall give him shall be in him a well of water springing up into everlasting life," and "whosoever will, let him take the water of life freely."

Knowing that the water in the glass but symbolizes this "living water" and that if we can in-drink the invis-ible we can also drink in the visible—for the visible but represents the invisible—I picked up the glass of water from the table, declaring, "Father, I thank thee, that thou hast heard me," put the spoonful of water to the patient's lips and *he swallowed naturally.*

This is enduring "as seeing him who is invisible" (Heb. 11:27). The spiritual way is the miracle-working way,

43

the way of quick deliverance, and the way of high vision transcends all planes beneath it.

In *Unity of Good* we read:

> An acknowledgment of the perfection of the infinite Unseen confers a power nothing else can. An incontestable point in divine Science is that because God is all, a realization of this fact … brings out the highest phenomena of the All-Mind … Man, in Science, is as perfect and immortal now, as when "the morning stars sang together, and all the Sons of God shouted for joy."

Hear the call of the risen Christ: Come, ye blessed! Stretch forth thy hand! Rise and walk! Thy sins are forgiven!

Such listening and such hearing is the wind that bloweth the chaff away. Such listening and such hearing is the divine ear that reports, "It is finished." Such listening and such hearing brings back the echo, "I have overcome the world."

Resistance, persistence, and insistence are of little value to us in our strong statements and high declaration unless our vision is toward the finished kingdom, toward the Maker of the universe, and we recognize and understand our infinite divinity: "I in thee, and thou in me."

There is no sickness, there is no lack, no loss, no inadequacy where the vision of God is. In order that we transcend our doubts, our fears, our erring thoughts, our limitations, we must look *above* doubts, fears, erring thoughts, and limitations. Miracle workers are they who believe in miracles. Are we going to let our gaze rest upon health, wealth, happiness? Are we going to be so in love with these "gifts of Thy love" that we forget to raise our gaze to the "Giver of gifts"? To the Health of our health? To the Life of our life? To the Joy of our joy?

O thou great invisible Omnipresence! I now identify myself with thyself. Thy strength is my strength. Thy abundance is my abundance. Thy might is my might. I am satisfied that I am awake in thy likeness; that I am filled with thy glory. I am satisfied that I am whole, that I am strong, that I am glorious, that I am free! All that thou art, that I am, O mighty, omnipotent, impersonal, and universal Truth!

Let us look now to the miracle workers, the prophets, and bring again into our remembrance the wonders they wrought, and let us discover how they wrought them.

Moses led the children of Israel safely through the Red Sea, and thereafter we find the "Song of Moses." "Who is like unto thee, O Lord? ... Who is like thee ... doing wonders?"

Bread and quail were sent from heaven, and water came forth from the rock. For forty years they were sustained in the wilderness and "lacked nothing," nor did their clothes and shoes "wax old."

"And the Lord spake unto Moses face to face, as a man speaketh unto his friend," and the name of God that was given to Moses was: I AM THAT I AM.

Elijah is fed by ravens; the widow's oil and meal are increased; the widow's son is raised; rain and fire are brought from heaven; and Elijah is translated and carried up to heaven.

In Psalms, we find a more extended account of the early miracles and miracle workers. David sings:

Marvelous things did he ... He divided the sea, and caused them to pass through ... He clave the rocks in the wilderness and gave them drink as out of the great depths ... He rained down manna upon them to eat, and man did eat angel's food.

He saved them from the hand of him that hated them and redeemed them from the hand of the enemy ...

> God delivereth Shadrach, Meshach, and Abednego from the burning fiery furnace ... upon whose bodies the fire had no power, nor was a hair of their head singed, nor the smell of fire on them.

No wonder they sang:

> Great is our God and who is like unto him, for he doeth things great and marvelous ... Which removeth the mountains, and hangeth the earth upon nothing ... Who maketh the clouds his chariot ... Before the mountains were brought forth, or ever thou hadst formed the earth and the world, even from everlasting to everlasting, thou art God.
>
> Acquaint now thyself with him and be at peace ... I will extend peace like a river and glory like a flowing stream ... To be spiritually minded is life and peace ... The kingdom of God is joy and peace.

Such peace as this restores the mind and adjusts the mental attitude to a right position. It makes no difference what conditions exist as the result of wrong thinking; there is a peace that is like a flowing stream, washing away all that is corrupt and undesirable. Remember, the universal God blesses the whole universe; the sun shines on the saint and sinner alike; on the good and on the bad, on the just and the unjust. The vision of the I AM is without partiality.

To have the view of the perfect One should be our aim, and this viewpoint blesses all. Herein do we find our freedom and our peace.

As we think rightly, and consequently manifest rightly, we are in tune with the *Isness* of Life; as we think wrongly, and manifest wrongly, we are out of tune, and that which we manifest is temporary and unreal. Now, one can have the true spiritual vision of Life as well as another, for it is God's free gift for all. Some of us may find ourselves achieving, progressing, and again may seem to stand still. Let us "Watch!" as said our Teacher.

The wheel of God moves swiftly on. It grinds by night and day. The worthless husks it drives from out the golden grain, the refuse from the flour ... True knowledge is the flour; false learning is the husk ... Be humble if thou wouldst attain to Wisdom ... Be humbler still when Wisdom thou hast mastered.

Be like the ocean which receives all streams and rivers. The ocean's mighty calm remains unmoved; it feels them not. Thou art enlightened. Choose thy way.

—Golden Precepts

A book that carries the tone of Spirit in its lines and is written from the inner plane is a treasure. It is like a well of water, always refreshing and inspiring, always upbuilding and illuminating. The Bible is so wonderfully inspirational because it circles around the fourth dimensional plane, and every time we read the miracles in the Old or New Testament, we find new gems of thought and healing.

We should live neither in the past nor in the future. The *now* is that which concerns us most, and the now is the eternal. Sometimes we take many steps before the Way opens up clearly to us, but after we have taken one— that is, fixed our inner vision in the right direction, toward the heights—other steps come naturally. Let us unite our vision, thinking, and feeling. Let us use our full nature to find the Self in Its full bloom. It is upward we are climbing, and it is upward that our vision should be transfixed. Looking downward will not enable us to make the upward climb; we may lose our foothold and again must retrace our steps. The sooner a mistake is seen, and corrected, the better it is for him who is climbing upward.

To be able to produce a certain result through conscious thinking is not the same as to demonstrate a principle through perception and understanding. In one instance, we depend upon the quality and quantity of our individual thoughts and feelings; whereas, in the other instance, we are depending upon our recognition of the free Spirit Itself. The first method is based upon a state of individual achievement; the last method is based upon a fixed, static Principle. The individual mind is always acquiring new ideas, but ever Spirit, the Christ within, remains the same.

Let those of us who thirst for living water and hunger for heavenly bread come closer to the divine Self—the living Christ. Let us "be still" so that the voice of this Christ may speak to us. Ever It promises:

> Behold, I freely give
> The living water; thirsty one,
> Look up, and drink, and live!

We speak to our Self or the Self of the one called patient:

> You know and I know that you are finished wholeness; that your life springs from the fountain of birthless and deathless Self-existence; that your health cometh from Him that maketh the heavens and the earth and holdeth the stars in their places.
>
> You know and I know that that which is, *is*. Nothing can change it; nothing can make it sick or weak or evil.
>
> You are peace, you are joy, you are power, you are glory. You are greater than all thoughts, greater than all things, greater than all trials, greater than all temptations, greater than all words.
>
> You are free Spirit, glorious, triumphant, and victorious. You are without trouble, without accident, without pain, without sickness.
>
> Arise! Manifest that which you everlastingly are, *the Christ of God*!

As we obey the command "Look unto me," our minds are filled with new ideas; our tongues speak a new language, and into our hearts is born a new hope.

How can Life cease to live when It is *everlasting*? How can eyes fail to see, ears fail to hear, lungs fail to breathe, or legs fail to walk when I AM is the power that causes them to *be?* Instead of keeping our vision on dim eyes or deaf ears or lame feet, let us place our vision on the Power that is changeless, constant, fixed—the Power that is back of the eyes and ears and lungs and feet!

> Since this Power is everlasting, I am everlasting. In the Everlasting I *was*, or I could not now *be*; so in the Everlasting I will remain forever, for the very reason that *I am*. Though mountains may move, though oceans may dry, and the whole universe fall into chaos, *I* remain forever within the folds of Life Everlasting.
>
> —A. K. Mozumdar

The inspired raise their inner sight to the universal Light, "that lighteth every man" beholding it. "As high as the heavens are above the earth, so are my thoughts higher than your thoughts, and my ways above your ways." Beholding the everywhere and ever-present completed splendor, illusions and erring thoughts are no longer remembered.

Jesus taught the eternal oneness of the individual with his Creator. This certainty of oneness, this feeling of unity, is the Spirit bearing witness.

The first person to need the quickening Spirit is the healer himself. In the spiritual way of healing, it is absolutely essential that the healer himself have an illumined mind, a consciousness of knowing, a certainty of feeling. Jesus was so filled with this great Soul light that the seekers had only to touch his clothes and they experienced healing. Should we put a lighted lamp into a dark room, everyone coming in contact with the light would automatically be lighted. And Jesus, the Beloved, was such a living flame of faith and understanding that those

49

who reached a state of spiritual contact with him by touching him were healed. Heavenly peace radiates from the presence of him who stands for the finished kingdom.

Believe that ye *have,* and ye shall manifest. Believe that you have all desires fulfilled—that is, believe that your desire is already fulfilled, and it shall be manifested to you in the mental plane. It is already fulfilled, already prepared, already manifested in the finished kingdom, in reality, and if one fixes the vision herein, the wish is manifested now and here.

As we become conscious of the grand truth that we *are* and that our perfection eternally *is,* our manifested life corresponds to this plane of conscious knowing. To know that all mind is mind of God, that all life is life of God, that all spirit is spirit of God, and to act and live from this viewpoint of consciousness is to light our minds with the sublime facts that automatically blaze our path.

We praise our wonderful free Self, the Self that is imperishable and glorious. We praise the great Universal, from whom all blessings flow. We praise the Selfhood of all who approach us for help and deliverance. We see the *one* Life, the *one* Christ, the *one* manifestation on all sides of us! Only such visions and such thoughts that uplift us eternally bless us.

If one is in mental darkness, he needs the light of intuition, the light of faith, to act as a ray to lift him upward. There is no lack; there is no loss; there is no luck. There is no failure in the spiritual plane. There is no new condition for us to manifest; there is no sickness over which we must demonstrate. There are no one's thoughts that harm us. As we act in the consciousness of our changeless freedom, our inherited perfection, our victorious Selfhood, this consciousness transcends the so-called laws of the lower planes. "The law of the Spirit of life in Christ Jesus hath made me free from the law of sin and death," announced the visioning Paul. The law of the spiritual plane is the law of the heavenly land and is the transcendent law of God.

To control the body through Spirit or through spiritual means takes a higher understanding of Life than to control it through mental means. Yet the mental means is a stepping-stone, not to be cast aside, for many mentalities can use the mental means successfully, where their understanding has not as yet sufficiently opened to discern the higher way. It is true that one can so train his mind as to consciously control his body; to suspend animation; to even live for a long time without eating or drinking. While this might well be thought wonderful, it really has little value except to prove what it is possible for mind to accomplish.

The high ideal is not one of laborious thinking, but is one of laborless action. Suppose one finds himself in sudden trouble, and his mind rushes forth with the question, "What shall I think to overcome this condition?" He consciously formulates some right thoughts like these: "I am feeling well … It never happened … I am fearless." Now, these thoughts arc good thoughts, right thoughts, true thoughts. But let us recognize a something that is of greater importance to us than even our right thoughts. It is our vision, our point of view, the point of attraction.

When one repeats over and over a right thought, like any of the above statements, is he not focusing attention to his *thoughts?* Is he not repeating the thought over and over with the aim that such repetition will manifest itself in the thing or state of bodily manifestation that he desires? Does he not believe that "since thoughts are things, I will think right thoughts about myself, and these thoughts will manifest as right conditions"?

For those who have not as yet left the realm of the physical and are watching their bodies and fearing people and things, the method of right thought proves most helpful and desirable. As one understands that in reality life is changelessly perfect, he fixes attention to that which *is* his health, that which *is* his harmony. He meditates upon Truth and declares Truth but fixes his vision to the Christ that is *above* sickness, above pain, above conditions. Right thought automatically follows high vision.

Let us be consistent. Let us claim the high point of understanding—perfect, changeless, unalterable perfection here and now—and let us know that our life is God Almighty; that our health is God Almighty; that our harmony is God Almighty, and this almighty Truth, recognized, is our deliverer!

Spiritual discernment holds thought to the great I AM; the ever-present Christ; the oneness of the individual with the Infinite.

To think in conformity with right vision is right. This is the right place for right thought to be. Illumination, intuition, inspiration, perception are of first importance, and as thought springs spontaneously from inspiration and illumination, it has the rich quality that one desires to experience. Always back and above, within and beyond us, is the infinite Life Itself, and it is this infinite Life that is expressing Itself in us and as us.

> Whatsoever God doeth, it shall be forever: nothing can be put to it, nor anything taken from it ... That which hath been is now; and that which is to be (manifested) hath already been.
> —Eccles. 3:14-15

"Think in conformity with absolute Truth" is the edict of the high plane. In reality, in the consciousness of God, in the kingdom of perfection and heaven, all good and all harmony is manifested now. We do not think this thought thereby to make it true to us; we think it because it is *already* true to us and because it is *independent* of our thinking. Our thinking has not a thing to do with the creation of the perfect. Our good already is created, and as we think in conformity with our already created good, we know even as we are known. "Known unto God are all his works from the beginning of the world." "As it was in the beginning, is now, and ever shall be." Health, joy, harmony, prosperity are already prepared for us, already manifested for us, in the finished kingdom.

In the spiritual way, we have the joyous feeling of laborless action. There is a thrill of peace and joy that comes over us from a hidden, inner spring; we marvel at the rest and peace we feel. It is the quickening Spirit, or the Spirit bearing witness.

Let us realize our kingship since the kingdom is within you. Can the beggar act as a king while he sees himself a beggar? Let us have kingly thoughts. It takes such thoughts, that we rest secure and peaceful. He of the high or kingly consciousness is not disturbed by any wind that bloweth.

It is the wooing warmth of the mother that brings the birdling from its shell. Thus is Spirit ever wooing us, uplifting us, beckoning us, calling, "Come, ye blessed, inherit the kingdom already prepared for you!"

Health is quiescent, still, back of all appearance of sickness as the sunshine is back of the clouds. We have a breath, a sight, a hearing, a feeling independent of the body or of the mind. Since we came forth from the one I AM, we therefore came forth with inherent wholeness which cannot be taken from nor added to us. To become conscious of the fact that we are free Spirit—unbounded, unlimited, undefilable, living, moving, breathing in the realm of omnipotent God—is joy-giving, health-bringing, peace-filling.

We bring that starry light to the eyes, that heavenly beam to the face, that thrill to the voice, as we have high vision and clear perception of reality. It takes the transcendent fire of Spirit to put live words into the mouth, inspiration within the heart, and sunshine into the presence.

We hear it said, "My sight is failing." Can the sight of the I AM grow dim or fail? Can the origin of sight be other than it was from "the beginning"? The substance that sees is God. This substance cannot grow old, aged, lost, or injured. It is as ancient as the Ancient of Days and as eternal as *everlasting* Eternity. Universal sight was before the individual became a conscious identity. That which is the origin of sight is changeless. The eyes *express* sight. The eyes and their outer vision symbolize God, Life, and Its ever ability to perceive and express Its own wonderful ideas. Thus, the inner vision of the perfect One remains inviolate, undefilable, changeless, and immortal. As we fix the inner gaze, the soul vision, the eye divine, upon these great facts of living Truth, we understand that our sight is God Almighty and is perfect and unfailing, sustained by heavenly law.

The same truth applies to hearing. We should not cut ourself off from high Truth, but we recognize our oneness with the all-hearing Whole and know: because Thou hearest, I hear! Whatever Thou art, I am that!

What greater power could we vision toward than that which is clothed in the garment of Omnipotence? What greater good could we desire than to have good that is ever-present? What greater joy could we hope for than to know we are walking now in the finished kingdom? As we fill our consciousness with this Light, so does this Light fill us.

Should we look to darkness instead of toward the light, what does darkness say to us? "Come unto me, and I will show you what I am and what I can do. Enter my presence, and I will prove myself to you, and you will not be able to see or feel anything but my presence, so great am I."

But lo, a hand pushing aside the curtains presses a tiny button in the wall, and where is the talking darkness? Gone—gone when the light comes into view. That which seems so big and appears so great an evil to us in an instant can be silenced into nothingness. But Truth cannot be thus silenced. Truth remaineth in sickness as in health, in poverty as in prosperity, in death as in life—the Self-existent I AM—the universal Absolute!

Does it make any difference to light how long the room has been in darkness, whether a single moment or a hundred years? It is all the same to the light. Let us not think or voice the idea that any difficulty is hard to overcome, hard to heal, or that any case will take a long time. These ideas have no place in the kingdom of finished wholeness.

The vision of wholeness is our bread of life and our well of living waters. Looking above shadows, we "lay hold upon the hope set before us" (Heb. 6:18).

We recognize the I AM as our everlasting health, our unchanging sight, our unalterable hearing, our unkillable life. Thus did Spirit vision Its own creation and pronounce, "Behold, it is very good!"

Who of us, while traveling in the mental journey from sense to Soul, have not had struggles, defeats, victories? As we learn the lesson, rise, and again press forward, we soon find that we have gained from the experience. We have learned more faith, more humility, more wisdom, more love. Testing times come to us all, from the least to the greatest, and blessed are we when we learn from them the lesson which they teach us. Thus reads the inspired hymn:

> Nearer, my God, to Thee, nearer to Thee!
> E'en though it be a cross that raiseth me.

Hear the ringing cry that came from the heart of the Master while in his greatest testing time: "O my Father, if it be possible, let this cup pass from me: nevertheless, not as I will, but as thou wilt." What do these words signify to you, to me? Jesus' desire was to give up the personal self and see with the high vision of our cosmic Father. There was nothing that he desired to change, but he knew that he must realize the indestructible Self and its at-one-ment with the great Infinite. And we know that whatever adjustment needed to be made in his consciousness during his great trial, he made it.

The divine Law takes not from us one good thing nor gives us one evil thing. The heavenly Law ever leads us towards the realization of our divinity, our own Godhood.

Some ask, "Why do I have trials? Why do I have such troubles, when I am striving so hard to think right?" It may be that such are living the plane of cause and effect, of action and reaction. We should not live in the thought of the body, that we are the body or that our body is physical or material. Rather, let us live in the consciousness that we are independent of the body; that we are divine; that we are Spirit; that we are above the planes of the pairs of opposites; that we are above the mental law of cause and effect.

Consider the rod which Moses told the people to look upon that they might be healed. Did the rod have power to heal?

"No," one replies, "but they thought that it had, and they were healed because of their thought. Therefore, thought is the healer or power."

But they could not think, were it not that they have mind with which to think!

"It is all the same," is the reply. "It was their own mind that had the power, and it was the power in their mind, or their mind was the power that healed them. Therefore, mind and its right thought is the healer."

But would they have mind and would mind have any ability or power to think if some greater power or some higher source had not brought this mind into being?

The individual mind did not originate itself. What is it that causes the individual mind to be able to think? The supernal One, the I AM THAT I AM. Hear the voice of this One:

> I am the first, and I am the last; and beside me there is no God. I, even I, am the Lord; I have made the earth, and created man upon it. I have stretched out the heavens. Look unto me, for I am God and there is none else.

After Peter and John had healed the man lame from birth, healed him instantaneously, the people were filled with wonder and amazement, and when Peter saw it, he answered unto the people, "Ye men of Israel, why marvel ye at this? Or, why look so earnestly on us, as though by our own power or holiness we made this man walk?"

The illumined Peter recognized that it was not by an individual power that the sick man was restored. And the Master, Jesus, what said he of his works? Whom did he glorify? It was after Jesus had healed a sick man and the multitudes saw it that "they marveled, and glorified God; who had given such power unto men." And Jesus said:

> To sit on my right hand and on my left hand is not mine to give; but it shall be given to them for whom it is prepared ... I seek not mine own will, but the will of the Father which hath sent me. If I bear witness of myself, my witness is not true ... There is another that beareth witness of me; and I know that the witness which he witnesseth of me is true ... For I came down from heaven, not to do mine own will, but the will of him that sent me ... Why callest thou me good? There is none good but one, that is, God.

If the immaculate Teacher gave glory to the universal Father and taught his disciples to be likewise minded, we understand that there is but *one* Power, and the power that we have to wink our eyelids and the power that we have to heal the sick is the one and same power—God Almighty.

By recognizing power as belonging to us the same as health belongs to us, we can have and claim all power, for did not Jesus claim, "All power in heaven and in earth is given unto me"? We can say the same, as we know it and prove it. It is well to note that Jesus proved this statement before he uttered it. It was one of the very last things he said to his students, and he said it after he had healed all manner of diseases, after he had raised three from the dead, and after he had raised himself from the dead. As we do this same work, we also can declare the same thing.

To speak the words "I am power; I can heal; I am health; I am understanding"—to speak these words as though we were speaking them from our own individuality as power—is one vision. To speak the same words because we know and feel our oneness with the great infinite ocean of Life is another vision.

Suppose a drop of water, resting alone in the bottom of a pail, said, "I am great. I am wonderful. I can sail big ships on my bosom. I can move great machinery. I am all-powerful, I am." Why, how foolish! It can do nothing at all but remain powerless in the bottom of the pail. But the drop *in* the great ocean can truthfully claim, "I am wonderful. I sail the ships. I carry the tons. I, in the ocean, have this great power!"

This is just what Jesus meant when he said, "I, of mine own self, can do nothing." And again, "All power is given unto me." We must take care that we do not talk like the drop of water in the pail, and let us be sure that we are thinking, "I, in the great infinite ocean of Almighty Power, can do all these right things." As we feel this union, this at-one-ment, as we feel the great reservoir back of us, we are not speaking boastfully; we are glorifying God.

"The Father is greater than I" signifies that we should recognize and glorify the sustaining Infinite back of the individual self and beyond the individual self.

> The sweet, sacred sense and permanence of man's unity with his Maker, in Science, illumines our present existence with the ever-presence and power of God.
>
> If man should say of the power to be perfect which he possesses, "I am the power," he would trespass upon divine Science, yield to material sense, and lose his power ...
>
> Who understands these sayings? He to whom ... divine Science unfolds omnipotence, that equips man with divine power ...
>
> Man should comprehend, in divine Science, a recognition of what the apostle meant when he said, "The Spirit itself beareth witness with our Spirit."
>
> The way is absolute divine Science: walk ye in it; but remember that Science is demonstrated by degrees, and our demonstration rises only as we rise in the scale of being.
>
> —Mary Baker Eddy

Thou great eternal Infinite,
Thou great unbounded whole,
Thy body is the Universe,
Thy Spirit is its soul;
If thou dost fill immensity,
If thou art All-in-All,
I am in Thee and Thou in me,
Or I'm not here at all.

How can I be outside of Thee,
When Thou fill earth and air?
There surely is no place for me,
Outside of everywhere;
If Thou art all,
If Thou dost fill immensity of space,
Then I'm in Thee and Thou in me,
Or else I have no place.

And, if I have no place at all,
What am I doing here?
Beyond the All, I cannot be,
Outside of everywhere;
Then truly, in Thyself am I,
And Thou must be in me,
Or else there is no All-in-All,
Nor Thee, nor me, to be.

But now I claim thy Spirit free,
Thy perfect Life and Soul,
The very thought of this great truth
Makes me this moment whole;
This very hour look I deep,
And vision high to see,
That Christ within—the perfect Self—
Art Thou! And I am Thee!

There is but one *I* expressing Itself in multitudinous particles of consciousness, and each particle of consciousness rests forever in the great infinite Whole.

Look to the All-seeing Presence! Speak to the All-hearing Substance! Know with the All-knowing Christ! And be ye steadfast and unmovable!

Resolve upon a certain spiritual right attitude of thought and maintain it. Keep thinking, feeling, knowing, and it comes to pass. This does not mean to think one way today and another way tomorrow, nor to have one idea this moment and change to another idea the next. We do not say, "This is Truth" now and the next instant wonder whether it really is Truth or not. Let us be firm and certain; steadfast and immovable! All that rightfully belongs to us is as fixed in the finished kingdom as the stars are fixed in the heavens. As our sense rises to divine heights, the body, environments, and conditions rise to correspond.

The weary one craves peace and rest, and where is it to be found? It is to be found in knowing and understanding the one Almighty Good; in knowing and understanding the real Selfhood, the Christ of God—in knowing and understanding the oneness of the individual Self with the Whole.

A son is a child until he grows into manhood. An individual in an unillumined and unenlightened state is a mental infant, knowing not the hidden mysteries within his bosom. But the mind wakens, true recognition and understanding takes place, and lo, the Christ is born again on earth!

Are we hearing the words of the miracle worker: "Labor not ... Lift up thine eyes to the fields already white to harvest ... Take no (labored) thought for your life"?

"But," exclaims one, "there is nothing good or bad but thinking makes it so, and we do experience what we think!"

Yes, this is true on the mental plane, but there is a heavenly law transcending the laws "as a man thinketh

in his heart, so is he" and "as ye sow, so shall ye reap."
It says, "Before they call, I will answer; and while they
are yet speaking, I will hear! ... Thy sins are forgiven
thee ... Thou art whole."

> And on the twelve-step ladder we ascend, until
> we reach the pinnacle of that which life is spent to
> build—the Temple of Perfected Man ... If you would
> see the Light, come to the Light ... lay aside all tense-
> ness of the mind, all fears, all doubts and troubled
> thoughts. Your human will must be absorbed by the
> divine; then you will come into a consciousness of
> holiness.
>
> —*The Aquarian Gospel*

Lift up the eyes to the finished kingdom. This was
the vision of the great triumphant, and this must be our
vision, that we do the works which he did—the marvels.
Those of us who are giving our life to preach the gospel,
heal the sick, cast out demons, raise the dead:

> Let us continue with strong commands to our great
> Self. Rise up, my Soul, and heal the sick wherever I
> walk! Show people how to be strong! Make people
> love God! Quicken me with heavenly fervor! Show
> me the finished kingdom through which I walk! Show
> me the words that make the world glad and sane.

Whether or not we believe that the world of four
dimensions is here, it is here nevertheless, but one must
look *up* if he would discern it. If one wishes the light of
understanding, he must look toward it, as light comes
not from below. Light comes from above.

Let us look, and look toward good, until we see good.
Let us get the view of the perfect One so fixed in our
hearts that we can look upon the sick and lo, the dark
phantoms of disease vanish under the glow of our blazing
light. Peter and John must have had this illumined sense,
for when they would heal the lame man, fastening their
eyes upon him, they said, "Look on us." Now, why should

they tell the man to look upon them unless they realized a Something within themselves glowing, bright?

We look to that which sustains health in order that we may be free from the beliefs of sickness. We look to the heavenly law of uninterrupted harmony that we may be free from the bondage of the sinner. High law of life frees us from the beliefs of sickness, sin, and death. High law is the transcending power that renders lifeless— null and void—every seeming law of the body and the mind that serves aught but the changeless Perfect.

It is by steadfastly facing Spirit that says, "I will not leave thee nor forsake thee," that we walk over the waters and through the fires and lions harm us not. "A thousand shall fall at thy side, and ten thousand at thy right hand, but it shall not come nigh thee"—one who is practicing the presence of God.

Recognize the present *Isness*! Face upward and away from the personal self! Plant the feet in the finished kingdom! Thus do we manifest right thoughts, right things, right conditions. Let our song be:

> I *have* the sight of God!
> I *have* the hearing of God!
> I *have* the feeling of God!
> I *have* the harmony of God!
> I *have* the health of God!
> I *have* the All of God!

The Red Sea opened up for Moses; the lions closed their mouths for Daniel; the iron gates swung apart for Peter; the storms ceased for Paul; the boiling oil had no harmful chemicals for John. We look upon lions and see lambs! We look upon Red Seas and see dry land! We look upon apparent sickness and see health! We look upon the apparent sinner and see the sinless! We look upon apparent failure and see victory! We look upon apparent death and see life! We have the vision of he who proclaimed, "All power in heaven and on earth is given unto me!"

> Grant me, O God, the "seeing eye,"
> The Spirit's vision, clear,
> That in the place of error's lie,
> The perfect may appear.

There is no idle moment for us visioning toward such achievement.

> Not forever by still waters
> Would we idly, quiet stay,
> But would smite the living fountains
> From the rocks along our way.
>
> —Lillie Bajee

It is the Spirit that quickeneth! Spirit is the real and the eternal! Steadfastly facing Thee, there is no evil on my pathway! Believe that ye have, and ye shall manifest!

This is the contagion of Truth. We have heard that on the lower plane there is a contagion of disease; we have heard that on the mental plane there is a contagion of thought; but how many of us understand and recognize that on the high plane there is a spiritual contagion—a contagion of heavenly good?

Many of us talk with individuals upon some particular problems of our own, and although we are very much in earnest, yet we feel that we do not receive that something for which we look. Again, we talk with other individuals and come away with the feeling of uplift, courage, faith, and joy. It is possible for one who has awakened the spiritual sense within himself to instantly detect whether another has this wakened spiritual sense or not. There is a touch of soul, a spark divine, that is as susceptible to the spiritually awakened as light and darkness are apparent to the outer senses.

You will recall how the disciples knew that it was Jesus after his resurrection. They did not recognize his face or his form, but their "hearts burned within them." As we talk with one who lights up something within ourself, whose words fall upon our inner hearing and cause something in us to respond and echo back—this is *spiritual* contagion.

Those who are highly spiritual do not even have to speak aloud; their very presence can be felt. If one is quickened himself, he knows as he talks to another whether he too is quickened or not. Jesus' consciousness was so aflame with living faith and light that those who were seeking help easily believed in him. When he said, "Do you believe that I can do this thing for you?" it was impossible for them to say no, for the light of his Spirit was already penetrating their darkness, and feeling this divine influence or contagion, they quickly answered, "Yes, I believe."

Peter, filled with the Holy Spirit, with inner zeal and inspiration, healed the sick and raised the dead and converted, in one day, three thousand people.

Now, the contagion that we feel and know by being in the presence of an individual who has the light can also be experienced from letters or from books. This is why a letter or a book lights up our vision, lifts our burden, and heals us. Words that touch us, stir us, are those with which we are in tune, those with which we are in rapport. If the writer is spiritually minded and we too desire the things of Spirit, this is an invisible link between us; we are imbibing impersonal and universal Truth through spiritual contagion.

As one light lights another, so one illumined consciousness may light another consciousness that is receptive.

Chapter III

CAST OUT DEMONS

"Repent and turn away your faces from all your abominations," counseled Ezekiel. "Repent ye, and believe the gospel" was the echoing admonition of the great Jesus.

Repentance, remission, and forgiveness are irrevocably joined. As we repent and forsake our wrong thinking and doing, our sins or mistakes are remitted and forgiven.

Habakkuk was visioning toward this high plane as he proclaimed, "Thou art of purer eyes than to behold evil, and canst not look on iniquity." So also was Master Jesus when he challenged the Jews: "Which of you convinceth me of sin?"

To the vision of the Perfect there is no sin. The vision of the Perfect beholds *no* evil. It sees Itself and Its manifestations as the all and the only. The way preparatory to this exalted view is the way of repentance, remission, and forgiveness. As we turn aside from the thoughts and things that keep us earthbound, and give for them right thoughts and right ways, we are reaching up to the heavenly viewpoint, and "he that humbleth himself shall be exalted" (Luke 14:11).

Sinful or erring thoughts and ways that are forsaken and repented are forgiven and remembered no more against the individual, who then shouts his liberty and his freedom. Wait not until you have reached the heights of health and holiness to shout victory, but shout victory and freedom as you are looking upward and *before* the demonstration is yet manifested. As we have a vivid sense of our Self as one with the I AM, a vivid sense of our Self as pure Spirit—Christ, the ideal man—we shout our victory, our freedom, our perfection, and what we proclaim ourselves as now being, that we *are* and that we manifest.

Let us lift up the mind from the temporal to the eternal, from the individual to the Universal, from the valley to the heights, from the seen to the Unseen, from death unto Life, and from sin and sickness to the risen Christ!

"My Father worketh hitherto, and I work." Back and above all individual consciousness and expression is the fountainhead, the infinite Life, the sustaining One. Recognizing this infinite Intelligence, Omnipotence, and Omnipresence, we feel capable of undertaking any task and accomplishing any achievement. Our desire is to bless all, to uplift all, to move steadily onward with the great cosmic Life.

The great man cares nothing for the homage of the world, cares nothing for the world's honor or praise, blame or censure. His vision is fixed on High, and his whole ambition and delight is to hold steadfast to this high vision. Many of us find that in giving up the personal self and in looking to impersonal and universal Truth, we come into a greater wealth of harmony and happiness. If it is necessary that we lose that which is holding us in the valley, let us rejoice to cast it aside, for better things await us.

As we do the right thing, walk in the right direction, say the right words, we are never troubled; our minds are peaceful, and we have a sense of freedom. As we do the wrong thing, say the wrong words, act the wrong action, we are troubled in our minds; we question, doubt, and wonder. Wrong feeling signifies to one that he is out of tune with universal order. We do right, and automatically we are in contact with universal harmony, the heavenly order.

On the mental plane, we find action and reaction, cause and effect, sin and punishment, and hear the mental law, "Whatsoever a man soweth, that shall he also reap." On the high plane of reality—the plane of the finished kingdom—we find Christ, the real Self, the God-Self, flawless, immaculate, sinless, spotless, undefilable. We hear the heavenly law:

> Though your sins be as scarlet, they shall be white as snow ... all sins shall be forgiven unto the sons of men, and blasphemies wherewith soever they shall blaspheme ... Behold, I make all things new ... And there shall be no more curse.

Let us not fear what people say, what people think, what the world believes. "Fear God and serve him." Know what is right and act it. If we can't, with one stroke, rise to the heights of freedom, we rise stroke by stroke, but we rise nevertheless. Subservience to doctrines we have outgrown is bondage; subservience to teachers, relatives, friends, or enemies is darkness and death. We serve the impersonal Christ of God! If we cannot take this position all at once, we take it step by step, but we take it nevertheless.

By recognizing all individuality as the cosmic Christ, we are free from ideas of personality and personal worshipping. Seeing God in everything and in everyone, there are no comparisons, no mine or thine. We are all living and loving, progressing onward and upward according to the Light that is shining for us all. This is a cosmic law, constantly operating for us individually as we put ourselves in contact with it.

> A mighty tide has risen. You are unable to resist this wave, which is sweeping away all priestly and Pharisaical doctrines ... If you want redemption, you must follow the kingdom's way—you must see everything in its natural perfection. By beholding

darkness, what do you gain? Nothing. You simply become unable to see the light.

It is time you followed the Master's injunction— the Jesus who always followed the inner guidance and inspiration; the Jesus who healed the sick and raised the dead; the Jesus who never compromised his vision; the Jesus who loved and died for the world. That Jesus is saying to you through the eternal Christ: "Seek ye first the kingdom of God, and his righteousness; and all things shall be added unto you."

—*The Mystery of the Kingdom*

Who of us has not found the Way difficult at times, dark and dreary, sad and lonely, painful and heartrending? Who of us has not risen from difficulties, stronger than before the trials? Trials and their overcoming lead upward. Real glory transcends those who feel the conquest of self. Difficulties are masters if we are slaves, and difficulties are slaves if we are masters. Many a one has lost his life because he compromised his vision; because he could not fall and rise, and fall and rise again.

Let us gain and hold the vision of universal freedom, which is greater than all erring thinking, greater than all sin, great enough to be victorious and triumphant over every difficulty. The higher we climb and the more expansive our vision the smaller appear the things beneath— the difficulties and obstructions. Solitude is good for the individual, as he feels contact with the infinite fountain of peace and harmony. It is in the quiet that we come to know ourselves. Fearing to be alone expresses to us the necessity of a more complete acquaintance with the all-loving Presence and the all-mighty Power. We love to go apart as did the Master, to commune, to meditate, to ascend. Silence and solitude hold no gloom or darkness for him who is companioning with the Christ of God.

Time is no factor in reducing sin and sickness to nothingness. It took but a moment's time by the world's clock-piece for deaf ears to open, blind eyes to see, and dead minds to spring from sepulchres as the healing Word was spoken. The time for all good is now. All of us must go forward until the goal of perfection is recognized, claimed, and manifested.

> O make me glad for every scalding tear,
> For hope deferred, ingratitude, disdain!
> Wait, and love more for every hate, and fear
> No ill—since God is good, and loss is gain.
>
> —Mary Baker Eddy

In this higher order of Life, we remember that we are always superior to our ideas, no matter what they are. No matter what we see, how we think, feel, or act, the real Self transcends all. This understanding is the rock under our feet; it brings us freedom and victory. This Truth raises our minds to the high plane of knowing, and we experience the harmony of that plane. As we view the Self as birthless, deathless, triumphant Spirit, above all ideas and realizations, above all thoughts and conditions, above all sins and punishments, we reach exalted view—the vision of the Self as the transcendental Christ of the finished kingdom!

I am free Spirit, glorious, adorable, undefilable, guiltless, ageless, deathless. I turn from all downward watch and look out and up to the hills—the Mount of Celestial Glory—and I behold the kingdom of transcendent joy. I see sinless joy and harmony flowing forth as a river of strength and gladness; I see finished wholeness, static, fixed, unalterable fact of God, *impossible of change*! And as I recognize this Truth and partake of it, I manifest it. As I in-drink and inbreathe this reality of Life, I am forgiven. I am satisfied, glorified, uplifted, and illumined; sins fall off, sickness drops away, doubt and uncertainty are gone. I see God as the soul of me. I arise whole, seeing with Thine eyes, hearing with Thine ears, knowing with

Thine understanding, O thou almighty, omnipotent and All-loving Life!

Our mind now expands into something larger than the contemplation of itself. We realize our relationship to *all* life. Back of every form of life is the universal I AM. We look at the grass, the birds, the sky, the air, the water and realize the oneness of All and the allness of One. We feel our relationship to the Whole and hear the words of the impersonal Christ:

> For if they did truly know Me, they would have no pride, would take no credit to or thought of themselves but would humbly abide in the consciousness of Me doing it all and would let Me and My impersonal love rule in every detail of their lives.

> In the Impersonal, *all* is one. When you can enter into the oneness of the impersonal consciousness and abide there at will, you have entered into My kingdom and have found God ... Having once entered this realm, you become one with Me and therefore one with all beings. I will feed you with the bread of the Spirit, and the wine of Life will flow through you in rivers of Living Love, blessing you in all ways and likewise blessing all whom you contact.

> If you will but abide in the consciousness of Me, the true Self within you, and let My holy, impersonal love abide in you and permit it to flow freely, unhindered, unconditioned from your heart to bless all whom you meet—if you will but do this, you may ask of Me *whatever you will*, and it shall be done for you.

> With only My love in your heart, My thoughts in your mind, and My life in your body, you will know I AM, your own true Self—for then there will be no other self.

Here is a method of vision, thought, and understanding that is very certain to cast out demons: In the beginning, God created ... what? *Ideas*—both simple and compound. The idea *finger* could be called a simple idea, while the idea *head* could be called a compound idea. The idea *six* is a simple idea, while the idea *six times six* is a compound idea. There is but one unit or idea in the whole universe, though there is infinite expression of this idea. The creation of divine ideas is forever complete in the finished kingdom. All ideas are true and changeless in the divine Mind that originated them.

Take the idea or unit *six*. Where is it? What keeps it? What holds it? We know that it is ever-present, on the mountaintop or in the valley. The weather does not affect it; birth and death never interfere with it; it cannot be sick or lost, unconscious or dead. The very same recognition applies to the head or lung or heart. The *idea* is the point of attention. If the idea is indestructible, unkillable, unspoilable, even so is its symbol.

This is high recognition. Instead of looking at the heart that seems to be out of order, look at the idea *heart* that divine Mind holds forever in the finished kingdom. The idea *head*, *lungs*, or *heart* cannot be sick, troubled, harmed, or dead. It is ever-present; it is undefilable, upheld by heavenly law. All God's ideas are indestructible; they cannot be harmed or touched by accident, disaster, sickness, sin, or death.

This was the correct view of Jesus when he beheld "the perfect man," thereby casting out demons. Insist courageously upon this grand fact of the finished creation—the omnipresence of that which is—and let attention be turned from appearances. This is the vision that blows away the chaff, that lifts the cloud, and behold!—here it is, that which was and which forever shall remain!

The substance of God cannot be diseased. The life of God cannot be dead. The Christ of God cannot sin. The mind of God cannot be deceived. The finished wholeness cannot be hid!

Light the mind with this vision and follow its light—the vision of unspoilable health, the vision of unkillable

72

life, the vision of revealed perfection, the vision of sinless Soul, the vision of the Christed self, *the vision of the finished kingdom*!

"Awake thou that sleepest," cried Paul. Command the self to waken; command the self of those whom you would heal to waken. Are we not walking through a redeemed kingdom? A healed world? A forgiven people?

The vision of the mental plane tells us that Jesus was the wayshower; that Jesus showed us the way in which we progress, heal, and redeem ourselves and others. In the mental realm, we discern that Jesus was working out his own salvation as he was rising from sense to Soul. High recognition brings us a clearer and deeper discernment of the great *opus* of Jesus and his great mission as the Messiah.

That Jesus was the divine Wayshower and that he demonstrated health, harmony, and life for others and for himself is true, but the still deeper meaning is that as visioned by the beloved John when he proclaimed, "And he is the propitiation for our sins; and not for ours only, but also for the sins of the whole world" (1 John 2:2).

The above quotation may need study and meditation that the deep, mystical meaning come forth, as also this:

> Himself took our infirmities, and bare our sicknesses. But he was wounded for our transgressions; he was bruised for our iniquities ... Repentance and remission of sins should be preached in his name among all nations ... Behold the lamb of God which taketh away the sin of the world; who gave himself for our sins that he might deliver us from the present evil world.

> For there is one God, and one mediator between God and man, the man Christ Jesus, who gave himself a ransom for all ... that he might redeem us from all iniquity ... that he, by the grace of God, should taste death for every man ... Herein is love, not that we

loved God, but that he loved us, and sent his Son to be the propitiation for our sins ... Unto him that loved us, and washed us from our sins ... and hath redeemed us to God out of every kindred and tongue and people and nation.

Did not this only Potentate (1 Tim. 6:15) triumphantly declare, "I have finished the work which thou gavest me to do"? And he uttered this before the betrayal, before the Crucifixion, before his apparent death, and before his resurrection and ascension. On the high mount of vision, Jesus beheld his finished work—the redeemed world, the forgiven people. Shall not his vision be our vision?

Does not this explain: "God sent forth his Son ... to redeem them that were under the law"? (Gal. 4:4-5). They who are under the law of sickness, they who are under the law of sin, they who are under the law of action and reaction—they are already redeemed by him who "obtained eternal redemption for us" (Heb. 9:12).

This is the vision of high watch! The vision of him who astonishingly announced to the sick man: "Son, thy sins be forgiven thee," and to the sinful woman, "Neither do I condemn thee."

Isaiah was looking toward this same height when he caught the message: "Though your sins be as scarlet, they shall be as white as snow." This high viewpoint is little understood and comprehended on earth today, yet this heavenly law of the finished kingdom is ever operative among us. Those who now grasp this deep significance need no longer feel the weight of mental cause and effect, but looking to the finished work, they can behold with the risen Christ the redeemed world, the forgiven universe, the free Self!

"Let us acknowledge the great and unprecedented and uncopiable achievement of Jesus of Nazareth who, by recognition of his own Soul, did the humanly impossible. He is the pivotal man. He is the Soul-bloom in the garden of man … We walk through a redeemed, healed, unpunishable world because of the vicarious suffering of Jesus of Nazareth who, being all Godhood, was and is forever Christ Jesus—God Jesus—the living manifestation of what man can do and be by recognition of his own sonship to Omnipotence."

In the Absolute, there is no sin and no consequence of sin. Did Jesus cry to his murderers, "You will suffer for doing this terrible deed"? No. Looking toward the summit of celestial glory, he beheld the divine law and saw them forgiven.

> Be true and list the voice within.
> Be true unto thy high ideal;
> Thy perfect self, that knows no sin;
> That Self that is the only real.
>
> —K.L.C.

The absolute unreality of sin, sickness, and death was revealed—a revelation that beams on mortal sense as the midnight sun shines over the Polar Sea … If the thought of sin could be possible in Deity, would Deity then be sinless? What is the cardinal point of difference in my metaphysical system? This: that by knowing *the unreality of disease, sin and death,* you demonstrate the allness of God …

When I have most clearly seen and most sensibly felt that the infinite recognizes no disease, this has not separated me from God, but so bound me to Him as to enable me to instantaneously heal a cancer which had eaten its way to the jugular vein. In the same spiritual condition I have been able to replace dislocated joints and raise the dying to instantaneous health.

—*Unity of Good*

It may seem strange to some that in knowing the unreality of a belief we demonstrate reality. This fine point is only comprehended in the Absolute. We bear in mind that we never have to make or create or cause to be that which already *is*. We have not a thing to do with the Absolute except to know that it *is*. But there seems to be a mist obscuring our vision and withholding the true and the real from us, and as we discern and understand the *unreality* of the belief called sin and sickness, which belief is the cloud or the mist, the real and the true which forever was and forever *is* becomes visible to us.

Thus, to understand the *allness* of the Perfect, and the perfect, manifested creation, is the vision that blows the cloud of sickness and sin away; and to know and to discern spiritually the unreality of the mist or cloud of sin and sickness reveals to us the perfect manifestation that is always present in divine Consciousness—the eye of God.

These are the "deep things of God" which are comprehended and understood in the stillness of meditation and consecrated vision. It takes spiritual discernment to comprehend this cardinal point.

A man was very ill; he also believed himself a sinner. As he lay meditating upon the law of Life, he thought to himself, "I have done a certain wrong; it is reacting upon me. I am now paying the penalty of that sin; I deserve the punishment." And he wept. Presently from out the storm came a still, small voice. It spoke with power and certainty: "No, I have not sinned. I cannot sin. I am as sinless as God."

That was all—but the transformation of the man! Instantly he recognized the high truth of God: Christ, the ideal Self, cannot sin, is forever above sin, above wrong thinking, above cause and effect! As this secret of the finished kingdom revealed itself to him, his mind and his body instantaneously responded, and he arose a perfectly well man. Two shall be in the field; one shall be taken, and the other left.

Another reports the following:

Four years ago my son-in-law made a financial venture and lost every cent. He had a wife and eight children. One of the boys had the worst temper ever known and was a terror to his family, and one of the little girls was paralyzed.

I went to them on a visit, and the following day while I was in my room reading, I heard a scream as if one of the children was terribly hurt. I hastened to find out the trouble. The little girl said, "Carl hit brother." At that, Carl hit his sister and knocked her down. I started for him, saying, "You wicked boy," intending to strike him myself, but a voice spoke to me, saying, "Overcome evil with good." I turned and went at once to my room and prayed for two hours as I never prayed before.

Then came the voice again: "Carl is healed!" In a moment I was calm and peaceful. I went to the mother and told her that her son would never give her any more trouble, and from that time to this, which is a period of several years, he has been the finest character you ever saw. The next day he applied for a position and developed into an electrician and is now overseeing four electrical plants in a large city. The little girl was healed of the paralysis, and when I came away they were all singing.

The slave of "things" is unable to perceive that his own thought is that which is controlling the thing. The slave of thought is unable to perceive that he, the thinker, is greater than his thought. The God-man is he who understands "*thine* is the power and the glory." As we realize that the Self of each individual is the one Selfhood, and that the power that is in us and the power that is in every other individual is the one Power, we have right vision, right thought, and right feeling. The recognition of the impersonal, immortal, sinless Selfhood is spiritual discernment.

To look to the perfect Self and recognize It as It truly is has healing influence and power and is the way of the finished kingdom.

Why struggle with thoughts and fears? Why not understand our own Nature? Our inherent success? Our established health? Our prepared good? There is in every individual that which is capable of being brought forth into the everyday life of that person as abundance of every good he may desire. The Spirit of the living God within us is the giver of all gifts. Universal God in us, the imminent, creative Omnipotence, is ready and willing to manifest at any moment, cast out demons, forgive our sins, renew our minds, our bodies, and our supplies. The certainty of the manifestation depends upon our ability to recognize this truth.

Let us take three cases. One recognizes God within as holiness, and in proportion to the recognition and trust with which this divine Presence is regarded, this man's life is pure and holy. He lives a holy life as naturally as a rose sends out its fragrance. But this holiness does not save him from sickness. Good people are often great sufferers and wonder why God "punishes" them. God does not punish anyone. As this man recognizes and accepts God as indwelling life—the life of his mind and the life of his body—then this divine Life, always perfect and strong, always ready to manifest Itself individually, is understood by him, and he is well and strong, the same as he is pure and holy.

Now, this man is pure and holy, well and strong, but he is very poor. Though he works hard and plans and prays for success, it is just the other way. What is the matter? The God within and without is abundance as well as health and holiness. There is no limit except as we make it by our lack of understanding. This good man, strong and well not long ago, because of failure in business started down to the river to drown himself. He was passing a church when a mighty current drew him in. He listened to the words: "If you are thirsty, I will give you drink; if hungry, I will feed you."

The man perceived real truth pertaining to universal supply for the first time in his life. Joy and peace filled him, and he went home a happy man. He said to his wife, "Where is the Bible?"

"Why," she said, "I sold it yesterday to buy milk for the baby."

With a face shining with light, he said, "Wife, I have learned at last that God is the great universal supply. All is well."

The next day a letter came to him containing money, and the following day came an offer of a splendid, lucrative position. Now he is a good, well, and prosperous man.

We do not look upon the "demons" sin, sickness, and death as though they were realities. There is no disease in the Absolute. The seeming difference between men is merely a difference in their states of recognition. To raise mind to the Christ-Consciousness is all that we have to do in order to rise above an abnormal condition. To get acquainted with universal Good, ever-present as universal right manifestation, is the divine panacea for all ills.

Elisha was a miracle worker. He increased the oil and the meal of a certain widow indefinitely, and when her son was sick and died, he took the child from his mother's arms and carried him to his own room and "cried unto the Lord, and said, O Lord my God, I pray thee, let this child's soul come into him again."

Paul was also able to raise the dead. He refused to believe that Eutychus was killed and told the people to "trouble not yourselves; for his life is in him." His vision was set to Life unkillable and imperishable.

The illumined Peter found a man named Aeneas, who had been in his bed for eight years sick of palsy. And Peter, filled with the vision of Jesus Christ, said unto him, "Aeneas, Jesus Christ maketh thee whole: arise! And he arose immediately." Then Peter was called to the house of Dorcas, who had died and was laid in an upper chamber, and Peter "kneeled down, and prayed; and turning him to the body said, Tabitha, arise … and he gave her his hand, and lifted her up."

"For whether is easier, to say, Thy sins be forgiven thee; or to say, Arise, and walk?" asked the comprehending Master. Let us be healers who forgive sin and give for it the joy of right living; let us set ourselves toward that illumination that casts out demons and raises the dead.

> The Way, the Truth, the Life—His Word—
> Are here, and now
> Christ's silent healing, heaven heard,
> Crowns the pale brow …
>
> Today, as oft—away from sin
> Christ summons thee!
> Truth pleads tonight: just take Me in!
> No mass for me!
>
> —Mary Baker Eddy

Jesus told us that "in the world, ye shall have tribulation; but be of good cheer; I have overcome the world." In illumined consciousness, the miracle of ascension is understood. Here demons are cast out and are no longer remembered. On the mount of transfiguration, pain and sickness are unknown, unfelt; herein the Christed self could no more be in pain than I AM Itself, nor can sin or poverty have any appearance, be either cause or effect.

A young girl was very poor, but she recognized the mystery of the finished kingdom and quickly grasped the heavenly law of "ask, and ye shall receive." She was an accomplished violinist and longed for a real violin to take the place of the cheap one she was using. Her vision was high; she felt certain that she could have the good that is promised. One night, she played in a hall, and played her cheap violin as though it were the actual instrument of her dreams. After the recital, a man came to her out of the audience and made her a present of his old violin, which was worth one thousand dollars, telling her how much he had enjoyed her great talent.

David sang, "God is our refuge ... therefore will not we fear, though the earth be removed, and though the mountains be carried into the midst of the sea." This is the attitude of faith that casts out the demons doubt, worry, fear, and discordant thinking. Without faith, the healing Word cannot bring forth its perfect results. The divine will for us all is wholeness and perfection. Knowing this Truth should keep us well, happy, and prosperous.

There is a lake in Switzerland so hemmed in by mountains that since the beginning of the world its peaceful waters have never been disturbed enough to cause even a ripple. Sleeping through eternity, its crystal bosom is glorified by sunbeams, while it delights in reflecting the glory of the heavens above it. What a wonderful lesson is this for you and for me. The real Selfhood, the Christ of God, is typified by this beautiful lake; only, the real man is even more securely protected. He is surrounded by Omnipotence, Omniscience, and omnipresent Love. From that moment when the words came forth, "Let us make man in our image," until now, the real man has ever been as undisturbed as has this lake in Switzerland.

> Just to keep our vision upward,
> Just to know that Love is here;
> Just to feel Truth's presence with us,
> Just to trust and have no fear.
>
> This is what "Our Father" wishes,
> This is what is asked of each;
> This is really all life's problem,
> This thro' faith we all may reach.
>
> Faith that knoweth Truth unchanging,
> Faith that listeneth to Its voice;
> Faith that easily commandeth:
> Rise! Come forth! Weep not! Rejoice!

We speak the word aloud. The spoken Word availeth much. Is it not promised: "While they are yet speaking, I will hear"?

Let us dismiss, with authority, the doubts that assail us and let us assert with kingly command the truths that *are*. Principle feels Its own perfection in the heart of the sinner as well as in the heart of the saint. Jesus came to us with the gospel of Love. He showed us the secret of the heavenly kingdom. He exhibited the Christ-Consciousness which holds all power. "And I, if I be lifted up, will draw all men unto me," uttered this Christ.

"They shall mount up with wings as eagles" is the promise. Lifted in consciousness, we find rise of power, and in Christ-Consciousness lies all power. This is the high goal, Christ-Consciousness! In this Consciousness we can command the demons to depart, and we do the things we are meant to accomplish. The world is awaiting this great impersonal and universal Christ-Consciousness.

> Go ye into all the world, and preach the gospel
> to every creature ... Heal the sick, cleanse the lepers,
> raise the dead, cast out demons ... Lo, I am with you
> alway, even unto the end of the world.

Chapter IV

RAISE THE DEAD

Many are asking, "What is the fourth dimension? What is cosmic Consciousness?" We have been taught that the world is three-dimensional, but in reality a dimension transcends length, breadth, and thickness. As a straight line is but the extension of the dot, so the fourth dimension of life is the *infinite extension* of all the other three dimensions.

Scientifically speaking, Life has no dimension, for how can that which is all have dimension or space? Four signifies unlimited direction—infinity.

There is a law within a law; there is a sight within a sight; there is a hearing within a hearing; there is a world within a world. There is a city that "lieth foursquare."

The fourth-dimensional world has timeless time and spaceless space. No time is herein, for all is the ever-present *now*; no space is here, for all is the forever *here*. This is the plane of birthless and deathless *Isness*. Here we need no light of the sun for radiance or heat, for the I AM THAT I AM is the light of the world and the glory thereof. It is the plane of Infinity, in which is nothing to obstruct, nothing to hinder; closed doors matter not; lions' mouths are of no account; tongues have no hurting power; prison bars or manacled wrists are as nothing.

The fourth-dimensional world is the plane of the miracle; the plane of the I AM; the plane of the risen Christ; the plane of the finished kingdom. It is the heavenly realm—the realm of heavenly law; the realm of ministering angels; the realm of quick deliverance; the realm of the Perfect Land.

Cosmic consciousness is the consciousness of universal good; the consciousness that sees God "face to face"; that talks with angels; that hears the "still small voice"; that recognizes I AM, the great Deliverer, the omnipotent Omnipresence, the birthless, deathless, causeless One—the Self-existent! This plane is not seen with outer eyes or heard with outer ears or recognized with the reasoning faculty. This plane is within us and above us.

Our great Teacher sometimes spoke of "the Father within," and again he spoke of "the Father above." The Christ kingdom is within the self, and it is also above the other cosmic planes. "Except a man be born from above he cannot see the kingdom of God ... I saw a light from heaven above the brightness of the sun ... Seek those things which are above ... Every perfect gift is from above." This realm has been called the supernatural or supernal realm because it is above the natural or apparent order of life.

Many who find satisfaction on the so-called material and mental planes believe impossible the things of above; they are foolishness to them because the above is unknown or not understood by them. This "above" realm has been called by some the mystical, as it is above the functions of the mind and holds the hidden secrets or mysteries of the kingdom of God.

One of my earliest demonstrations of reality gave me an experience of cosmic Consciousness. I had accepted a position as teacher in a public school. A few days later, the principal stepped into my room and asked me when I would be ready to take charge of the music. What was my amazement to discover, upon further conversation, that I was expected to play the piano each day for the morning assembly of all the children in the school. This meant marches and songs—*and I knew not how to play.*

It seemed that I had signed the contract without notic-
ing this requirement. I did not divulge my inability to
play, but asked a few days' grace, which was granted me,
and I was scheduled to begin the work on the following
Monday morning. That night, I thought it all over and
concluded that since the position had come to me because
of my application of Truth, then there was a way in
which I would be able to fulfill all requirements. What
kind of truth would it be that would bring a right and
desired thing to one and not make it possible for that
one to perform his duties?

The problem did not seem too hard or too difficult.
Certainly I could conceive of nothing impossible! Thus
it was that the first thought out of the difficulty was
this: buy a march and practice it. That night, after all in
the house had retired, I crept quietly into the living room,
placed my newly acquired march before me and seated
myself at the piano. It meant nothing to me. The notes
were like so many Greek figures, and my fingers were
the same as little sticks. It was absolutely impossible;
the mental plane, the method of thinking I could do it,
was not sufficient for this problem.

I sat still at the piano for several minutes until a ray
of light came to me from *within*. It was this: there is only
one way in which this difficulty can be surmounted. It is
the way of faith. Have faith. Have faith in the Almighty
Power Itself, and It will fulfill Itself in you. Unhesitat-
ingly I answered, "I will."

The following day was Sunday. I never looked at the
march; never gave it a thought nor went to the piano. I
spent the day in reading the Bible and books of spiritual
nature. I read that *nothing is impossible to him who
believes*. There was not an individual with whom I might
speak of this task before me; I was in a strange city, with

strange people. But all day I companioned with universal God. When Monday morning arrived, I was in a peaceful and uplifted state. Picking up the Bible to read one last verse to carry with me in my trial, this was the verse that met my eager eyes:

> Have not I commanded thee? Be strong and of a good courage; be not afraid, neither be thou dismayed … I will not fail thee nor forsake thee (Josh. 1:5, 9).

I walked on the very air over to the school building, my march held tightly in my hand, my gaze fixed high.

It was the custom for all the teachers to be seated in the assembly hall, and the sounding of the gong was the signal for the music to begin. The gong sounded. Then the wonderful thing happened to me! All thought completely left me; I arose and walked toward the piano, while children, teachers, myself, all seemed blotted out of my vision.

As in a dream, I placed the march before me and lifted my hands to the keys. At once, my fingers found the right notes as though they were hands other than mine; the music came, the children marched. In the same way, I played several songs that were announced, and again replayed the march as the children returned to their respective rooms. As I struck the last note, I emerged from the state of cosmic Consciousness and became the self of this plane again.

Little did I then understand that I had reached a plane of consciousness where mind is governed by heavenly law and need not be taught. I had touched the All-knowing plane; here knowledge is ever-present. Jesus did not attend schools and colleges; he knew without this. He knew more than all his teachers. The Christ of God is ever all-knowing.

"Two are ever in the field." This experience took the Christ of me and left the other. I took charge of the music for two years in that school.

Many have asked, "Did not the thought come, 'Suppose I fail? Suppose I cannot play after I take my place at the piano?' " I can truthfully say such suggestions never came into my mind. I was not looking to myself to do the playing, because I knew I could not. I had clear vision—the vision of the One able-to-do-all-things; I had absolute faith, and behold—the miracle. Reason can never attain to the heights of simple faith and child-like trust in the universal Executive.

Now, faith in ever-present Omnipotence above us, as within us, is not blind faith. Faith in a power outside the individual self as individual power is not blind faith. It makes no difference whether we vision power as within us, the Christ, or as above us, the Universal. It is all the same Power.

"Act as though I were, and thou shalt know I am." This was what I did. I not only believed, but I *acted*. Standing before hundreds of faces, fearless and victorious, facing up to One who ever says, "Fear not! *I* will not fail thee nor forsake thee. Be thou strong and very courageous, for thy Self is Myself—*I* in thee, and thou in Me."

The plane of the fourth dimension is here and now. "But," it is objected, "we do not see it; we do not feel it; we do not comprehend it."

Where is our vision? Are we visioned toward it? Are we believing in it? Have we had faith in it? How many are looking to books and teachers, to laws and authorities, to money and houses, to things and thoughts, to relatives and friends, to the dead past and to the living-dead spirits? How many are looking to the great Unseen, the invisible plane, as one expectant, watchful? "And when ye see this, your heart shall rejoice" (Isa. 66:14).

Can we view the valley and look toward the heights at the same time? Can we draw out health while our vision is set toward sickness? Can we hear the still, small voice while earthquakes and storms are raging within us? Can we find the Christ while we are wondering where the Christ is located?—whether It is within me or without me, above me or around me? Do I live in Christ, or does Christ live in me?

"Why reason ye?" Why strain and labor and analyze? Does the fish question, "What keeps me alive? Is it the water within me or the water without me?" Does the flower question, "Why do I have to look up in order to grow up?" Do you suppose Daniel argued with himself, "What shall I do if the lions do come toward me?" Did Moses pause, while passing through the Red Sea, to think, "Suppose the waters come together before we reach the shore?" Did Peter, bound with chains in the guarded prison reason, "How shall I *think*, that I may break these chains, put these soldiers to sleep, open the iron-bolted gates, and escape unnoticed?"

Vision must be set to the highest; the eye must be single and the faith supreme, that we experience the marvels of Truth. To the I AM, the here and the there are the same; the past and the future are the *now*; the above and the below, the right and the left, the up and the down, the inner and outer are *one* Presence, *one* All!

Even in hell, is not God there? Is not the Ever-present *everywhere*? Did not the Creator make both the "inside" and the "outside"? Wherever we look for God, there God is—whether in the sky or in the bottom of the ocean; whether in the air or above the air; whether in the past or in the future; whether on this plane or on the next; whether within us or without us. Lo, God is All-in-all, the high and the low, the here and the there, the in and the out, the up and the down, the visible and the invisible, the seen and the unseen!

Can we locate our mentality? Can we locate our soul? Can we locate the power that makes our heart beat? Can we locate the power that winks our eyelids? Can we locate the power that causes us to be? Can we locate the Christ within us or without us? Do we reason, "It is over my head; in front of me; at my right side; at my left side; before me; behind me?" Will this reasoning take us to the heights? Will this reasoning show us the finished kingdom? And does it matter where—when all where is *here* and all there is *now*; all to be *is*, all future *has been*, and all that is, *was*; all that is without us is within us, and all that is within us is without us?

Let him who thinketh there is a "within" (individual) God, but there is no "without" (universal) God, search the inspired Word more carefully. Let him who thinketh there is a "without" (universal) God, but there is no "within" (individual Christ of) God, enlarge and illumine his knowing. Is not God *one* God? Is not the one God the All-God? Can there be any within and without to that which is All? Let us have a care that we do not swallow camels while we strain out gnats, and let us hear and meditate upon the words of the Morning Star: "Ye fools, did not he that made that which is without make that which is within also?" (Luke 11:40).

He of high watch announced, "The wind bloweth where it listeth, and thou hearest the sound thereof, but canst not tell whence it cometh, and whither it goeth" (John 3:8.)

It was the beloved disciple, the revelator of divine things, who proclaimed, "And the length is as large as the breadth; the length and the breadth and the height are equal … I am Alpha and Omega, the beginning and the ending, the first and the last."

Let us cease locating the I AM, and wherever we look, let us know *there* is the I AM! There are many in the past history of the world who have had touches of the fourth dimension—the realm of no restrictions, the realm of the miracle, the realm of ministering angels. Daniel said, "My God hath sent his angels and hath shut the lions' mouths." And when Peter was put between two soldiers in the prison and bound with chains, "Lo, the angel of the Lord came upon him, and a light shined in the prison … and his chains fell off from his hands; the iron gate opened to them of his own accord … and the angel departed from him" (Acts 12:7, 10).

The books of the Old Testament are filled with chronicles of ministering angels, and great ones tell us of seeing angels, speaking with angels, seeing their great light. Those who have themselves heard the voice, seen the light, felt the touch, know and understand. In our own time, many have been the remarkable instances and experiences attending white light. Soldiers on the battlefields saw and felt it.

A friend from North Carolina writes that after years of both mental and bodily suffering from troubles for which there seemed to be no relief, "death, that great nightmare of the phantom world," came to claim him. At that moment, he was suddenly lifted into the plane above and recognized the nothingness of death. Directly over the head of his bed rested a great halo of a brilliant, soft light, brighter than any electric light he had ever beheld.

He declares there was a spiritual or supernal force in the room that was irresistible, drawing him up and on, and making clear to him that in reality he had never been sick; that he lived, moved, and had his being in God's kingdom right here and now; that this is Life's glorious city of New Jerusalem. The room seemed filled with the "water of Life," flowing in every direction and filling his consciousness with divine joy and inspiration. Then the vision ceased; he opened his eyes, knew that he was healed, and arose from what had seemed his deathbed, whole. He declared that for days afterward he felt as though he were walking on air, he seemed so light and free and glorious.

A London magazine contains the following account of a miraculous healing:

> Friends and neighbors of Dorothy Kerin of Herne Hill, London gathered at her deathbed. The doctors said she could not live until morning. During the last fortnight, she never moved her position, was blind and deaf and unconscious. She had been confined to her bed for five years, had been attended by twenty-eight doctors, and turned out of the hospitals "incurable." Such was her condition, and the end had come. As mother and friends stood near, she seemed to breathe her last. For eight minutes her lungs ceased to breathe, and her heart ceased to beat, and they deemed her dead.

> But at this moment, Dorothy declares, someone called her by her name three times. She replied, "Yes, I am listening. Who is it?" And the voice said, "Listen." Then she saw a wonderful white light, and it came right over her bed. In the midst of the light stood an angel, who took her by her two hands and lifted her up, saying, "Dorothy; your sufferings are over. Get up and walk." She then opened her eyes and, seeing her relatives about her, said, "Give me my dressing gown, I want to walk."

> They tried to hold her to the bed, but she firmly pushed them aside and, with eyes and ears opened, rose and walked. "I feel as though I would like some supper," she said presently. After some reluctance, they brought her something to eat, and she ate it in the presence of them all, and to their great astonishment.

The magazine further tells that crowds of people then came to see Dorothy. She interviewed sixty people the first day and one hundred people the second day. Doctors took X-ray photographs of her body and found that instead of the two old wasted lungs, there were two quite new ones in their stead and that she was every whit whole.

The age of miracles is not past, but lo, heaven and miracles are still here for those who are watching for them. "God is no respecter of persons." Truth is the same yesterday, today, and forever. This high state of consciousness is possible to all men. In this state, the true man, the perfect man, comes forth. Such illumination transcends the mind and its process of thinking. In no sense does one lose his identity. Rather does he *know* his identity. Such states of illumination are called cosmic Consciousness.

Several years ago, according to the law of the lower planes, my child could be taken from me to the house of "abominations" because she was considered, upon medical examination, contaminated. I was granted twelve hours in which to heal her through spiritual means. Alone, in the silent watches of the night, I read in the Book of Life: "A thousand shall fall at thy side, and ten thousand at thy right hand; but it shall not come nigh thee." Who? They who look up to the most High; they who have the "faith of God."

All unconsciously, I obeyed the science of the high plane, the plane of Spirit. I looked up; I reached up; I beheld God and perfection as the *All* and the *Only*. I saw no sick child; I saw no doctors; I saw no hospital. I saw the finished kingdom and the angels, which are promised, and I believed. Presently great peace came to me, and I thought, "Oh, if only an angel would come and talk to me, as is recorded in Bible times." How I yearned for a sign to convince me that "All is well." I opened the Book of Life, and my eyes fell upon these words: "And the Lord sent his angel, saying, I have heard thy prayer." This was enough. I closed the book. Nothing now mattered. I was in absolute peace.

In the morning they came; they examined. They said, "The conditions are the same, no change. We must take the child." Then the wonderful thing happened! The super-mental, the *above* world, came down to my sense, transcended the plane upon which I stood, and lo, semi-circled around me and behind me, from the right hand to the left, I saw, I felt, I heard a host of angels. "Fear not," was what they said.

What was seen and felt could not be put in writing. I stood unafraid. Those before me took their eyes off the so-called material plane long enough to look at me, and beyond me. What they saw, I know not. Suffice it to say, they reached for their hats and quietly left the room and house, and the child was instantaneously healed.

Sacred as these things are, they must be told that others may see that the "impossible" is possible; that the supernatural is divinely natural; that the realm of the miracle is here and now; that the heavenly law transcends all.

At another time, during the recent war, I spent several weeks in studying the 23rd Psalm, that I might write it in ringing tones for the soldiers. In this Psalm, I saw God, the I AM, as the great Deliverer, the Able-to-do-all-things. I will quote the little verse I sent out in print across the seas:

> I shall fear no evil. Thou, Truth and Love, surround and protect me. Thy rod, the denial of evil's power, and Thy staff, the affirmation of divine Truth, they comfort and deliver me. E'en though the shadow called death is 'round and about me, I shall not be afraid of it, for I know that I live in Spirit, which is indestructible and deathless. The consciousness of the ever-presence of divine Love and Wisdom constantly pro-

tects me from all harm and danger, and I realize that I am housed in God, where no evil shall come nigh me.

During the time that this was so fresh and filled all space in my consciousness, one evening I stepped into my car and started down the avenue. It was a very dark night, and I neglected to turn on my headlights. I had showing only the small dimmers. For the first time in my experience while driving a car, I forgot all about the driving, forgot what I was doing or where I was going. I was thinking only of this verse that I was getting ready for the soldiers.

All of a sudden I came back to "earth," to find myself in a seemingly great and irresistible danger. I was going at a terrific rate of speed, and my car was entirely out of my control. On the left-hand side of the avenue, directly before my terrific speed, stood a horse and a wagon with one occupant. I could clearly see the red light that was carried on the wagon, and no doubt the driver, seeing me coming toward him at my uncontrolled rate of speed, had pulled his horse as far as he could to his right-hand side of the street.

Nothing on the lower planes of life could save me now. There was but one way out. This way was the way of the miracle, the transcending fourth dimension. I did not *think* a thing—I did not have time. I did not *do* a thing—I couldn't. But had not I been looking up to the great Deliverer, the Able-to-do-all-things?

In a twinkling of an eye, lo, all was changed. I felt myself, in the car, moving as through the air. I entered the plane *above*, and I was distinctly conscious of passing through the horse and wagon, which were like a cloud, a mist or vapor. The glory and joy of it are too great to tell, for all that read these pages may not have the "hearing ear." I was also conscious when I had passed through the horse and wagon, for I came out into clear space, open and free, and I traveled in this free space for some time; then there was a quiet return to the natural order again. The car seemed to float from the air down to the earth, and I found myself in the center of the street a half mile from the spot in which the "miracle" took place and my car moving as though I had just started it.

The victorious Jesus worked on a plane above the three-dimensional plane. Where was the law of weight and strength when the stone rolled away and the grave opened up? Where was the law of time and place when he stepped into the ship and was directly found on the other side? Where was the law of limitation when he took three loaves and two small fishes and, looking up, fed the multitude with abundance?

Jesus lived on a plane in which is spaceless space, in which is nothing to oppose. Facing the Father, he said, "I thank thee, and I know that thou hearest me always." Then from this plane of consciousness, he saw the living Lazarus and called to him, "Come forth!" He did not see blind men or deaf men or dying men. He had the vision of the perfect always within himself, and from this plane of changeless perfection he commanded: See! Hear! Come forth! Rise and walk!

We think nothing at all of commanding the child to "Run upstairs" or, "Come to me" or, "Close the door." We know the child can do it; hence the command.

A woman attended services at a church one night, taking with her a son, about twelve years of age, who was subject to what is called epilepsy. During the service, the boy was overcome by an attack of illness and was carried into another room. The mother was asked if she would like to have her boy "treated," and not knowing of what this consisted but with the idea that it would be helpful, she replied, "Yes." When the boy recovered, the practitioner said to him, "Repeat after me: I am God's perfect child." The boy made no reply. The practitioner repeated his request, but still the boy made no attempt to obey. The practitioner then put his hand upon the boy's shoulder and *commanded* the boy, "Say after me: I am God's perfect child." The boy then spoke as directed.

Now, the mother of the boy, who was listening as though spellbound, fainted. When recovered, she exclaimed, "Those are the first words George ever spoke. He was born dumb!" The practitioner did not know that the boy was dumb when he told him to speak; he believed the boy *could* speak, and acting upon the healer's command, the Christ of the boy responded. Believe that ye *have*, and ye shall *manifest*.

Within and above the cocoon is the butterfly; within and above the acorn is the oak; within and above the three-dimensional world is the city that lieth four-square, the city New Jerusalem, that needs neither the light of the sun nor stars; that holds no sorrow or tears. Herein is no lack or loss; herein is no evil, no power that can harm; herein the lion and the lamb lie down together, and Love divine rules over all.

"And the city lieth four-square, and the length is as large as the breadth ... the length and the breadth and the height of it are equal" (Rev. 21:16). That which *is*, forever is the same. The "city" signifies Truth, always and forever the same from every side we view it—the changeless, the static, the immovable; the Truth that *is*. *The city that lieth foursquare is the finished kingdom.*

> This sacred city, described in the Apocalypse as one that "lieth foursquare" and cometh "down from God out of heaven," represents the light and glory of divine Science ...
>
> This heavenly city, lighted by the Sun of Right-eousness—this New Jerusalem, this infinite All, which to us seems hidden in the mist of remoteness—reached

St. John's vision while yet he tabernacled with mortals. The builder and maker of this New Jerusalem is God ...

This city is wholly spiritual, as its four sides indicate ... It is indeed a city of the Spirit, fair, royal, and square ...

This city of our God has no need of sun or satellite, for Love is the light of it, and divine Mind is its own interpreter. All who are saved must walk in this light.

—*Science and Health*

Why expect death to bring us these wonders? Why not experience them now? Water cleanses the body; right thoughts purify the mind. Love and illumination, meekness and might, faith and confidence to command is the path of the Soul, the path of the ever-present fourth dimension.

In the land of fadeless day,
Lies the city four-square;
It shall never pass away,
And there is no night there.

God shall wipe away all tears:
There's no death, no pain, nor fears;
And they count not time by years,
For there is no night there.

All the gates of pearl are made
In the city four-square;
All the streets with gold are laid,
And there is no night there.

And the gates shall never close
To the city four-square;
There life's crystal river flows,
And there is no night there.

There they need no sunshine bright,
In that city four-square,
For the Lamb is all the light,
And there is no night there.

—John R. Clements

97

As we rise in the scale of Being, naturally we experience heavenly things and divine illuminations. The illuminati find it hard to express or write about "unseen things above," for the foolish-minded would defile it. High recognition does not spring from any organization of thought, but from the mount of vision.

The kingdom of heaven is *within* us. Do we believe it? Do we claim it? Do we acknowledge it? Do we praise it? As heaven is within us, then *perfection* is within us. Light the mind with this truth and follow its vision. Following this high view, we behold that the *above* body is within us. The *above* body is the spiritual body; the eternal body; the immaculate body; the birthless and deathless body; the body that is never touched by pain, harmed by accidents, devoured by lions, or bitten by serpents. Lo, the body of this kingdom is greater than the fire, for fire cannot burn it; it is greater than the water, for water cannot drown it; it is greater than the prison bars, for prison bars cannot hold it; it is greater than sickness, for sickness is unknown to it. It is greater than death, for death never reaches it.

The idea of death is a universal belief that must be set aside as we realize our birthless and deathless being. Soul is God, which always was and always shall be. Life, Soul, Spirit, is not born, nor does It die.

> Never the spirit was born,
> The spirit shall cease to be never;
> Never was time it was not,
> End and beginning are dreams!
> Birthless and deathless and changeless
> Remaineth the spirit forever;
> Death hath not touched it at all,
> Dead though the house of it seems!
> —*The Bhagavad-Gita*

Oh, wonderful, glorious body of God—the body that God pronounced good and perfect!

Paul tells us that there is a natural body and there is a spiritual, or supernatural, body. There is a body belonging to the earthly plane, and there is a body belonging to the heavenly plane. Place the vision upon the spiritual body, the transcendental body, the body belonging to the fourth dimension. *It is already prepared for us.* "The flesh profiteth nothing." They who live in the consciousness of the body of flesh and bone live in the consciousness of sickness and death. "Flesh and blood cannot inherit the kingdom of God ... They that are in the flesh cannot please God ... Walk in the Spirit." Keep the vision away from the body of the three-dimensional world and recognize, claim, and acknowledge the supernal body, for "that which is born of the Spirit is spirit."

With what body did Jesus pass through the walls and doors? With what body did he walk over the water? With what body did he come from the grave? With what body did the three Hebrews live in the fire? With what body did John live in the boiling oil? With what body did Dorothy rise from her deathbed? With what body did I pass through the horse, wagon, and man? *With the body that is ever-present, above; within the body that is already prepared for us.*

Listen to the Word of Life: 'That which hath been is now; and that which is to be hath already been ... Thy hands have made me and fashioned me ... in thy book all my members were written ... when as yet there was none of them."

The body of the heavenly is the first and the last— that which hath been is *now.*

"For this corruptible must put on incorruption, and this mortal must put on immortality." When? *Now.*

"Turn ye now from the evil of your doings, and dwell in the land that the Lord hath given unto you ... The hour cometh and now is when the dead shall hear the voice of the Son of God, and they that hear shall live ... Now it is high time to awake out of sleep ... Now is the day of salvation. Now are we the sons of God: Behold, now is the accepted time." *Light the mind with this Truth and follow its vision!*

Christ Jesus was the great ambassador of the finished kingdom. He represented the *now*. He stood for the *real*—the ever-present Unseen. He said:

> Everyone that is of the Truth heareth my voice ... I am come a light into the world, that whosoever believeth on me should not abide in darkness ... I am from above ... I am not of this world ... It is given unto you to know the mysteries of the kingdom of heaven ... And as ye go, preach, saying, the kingdom of heaven is at hand.

It was St. Paul who declared, "There is one body and one Spirit." Then have we not a body the same as that which Jesus had? The body that can pass through walls unharmed, stand upon the water and not drown, "shine as the sun," come forth from the tomb and live, be carried up into the heavenly plane?

Most certainly we have. Where is it? It is already prepared for us. It is ever-present, waiting our recognition. At any moment, a touch of cosmic Consciousness, the fourth-dimensional kingdom, may reveal it unto us.

Therefore, said the Master, "Watch!"

Chapter V

JESUS CHRIST

Jesus told in different ways, to make it clear to his listeners, that the Father dwells without us as well as within us; that the divine *I* of us is this Father, and that the Father is He that doeth the healing works.

As it was difficult for students directly under the Master of teachers to understand this high teaching, it is not to be wondered that in the present day we find the same condition. It is foolish for us to think of the individual self as being powerful and great, for we could not as much as breathe were it not for the power back of us. God, the I AM, is this power! This infinite Ever-present is the one Power that acts in all living things throughout the universe; thus, we recognize that we would not even be, were it not for this Power that is behind us and beyond us.

The same Jesus Christ is in us that was in the lowly Nazarene—the same life, the same power. "The word that ye hear is not mine (the personal me), but the Father's, which sent me … He that hath seen me hath seen the Father." Recognizing the Christ-Self of any individual, we are beholding the Father, for the Christ-Self and the Father are *one*. The Christ (as the individual) and the Father (as the universal) are the same substance. "I can of mine own self do nothing." The individual self cannot do the works of God except he recognize himself and the Father as *identical*.

"The works that I do, ye shall do also" because the same Christ dwells in you as dwells in me, taught the Master. God is no respecter of persons; each Self is a particle of the omnipresent All, each Christ the same in glory. Think in the universal! "Ye are the light of the world."

Jesus, the Beloved, never compromised his vision. He would not allow even grateful hearts to call him good, but he turned their attention away from himself and pointed to the One great; the source of his greatness. Look to this I AM was his edict.

Some churches have little to say of Jesus Christ; some churches have much to say about Jesus Christ. They tell of his sorrow, his betrayal—how even his disciples left him alone on the high watch; how he was crucified and how he died for us. What shall *we* tell? Where shall *our* vision be? *To the risen Christ!*

Our vision is to Jesus Christ, who overcame death; who walked and talked, ate and drank with his disciples after his resurrection! To the Jesus who said, "What I say unto you, I say unto you all, Watch." To the Jesus who said, "Go ye into all the world, and preach the gospel … heal the sick, cast out demons, raise the dead," and *I*, the risen Christ, "am with you alway."

Jesus was the great prototype, the perfect example, the victorious Christ. Did not he show us plainly the divinity of the Self? Did not he show us how to think in the universal? The same Spirit dwells in you and me as dwelt in him. There is but one Jesus Christ—and that is the I AM that is in you and in me.

Jesus Christ as Emmanuel, God with us, is the true Self, the divinity of us, the perfect man. This is the universal Christ. This is the cosmic Christ. This is the Christ of God!

Let us suppose that a handful of diamonds is lying in the dirt. They are covered with mud and layer upon layer of soot and slime; some are black, some are brown; some are one shape, some are another. As they are gathered together, lo, there comes into their midst a flaming white light, a magnificent white stone, which sparkles and dazzles and is brighter than the sun.

They have never seen such a stone before, nor even heard that there was such a marvelous stone. Little do they dream that each one of them, each separate ball of dirt, is at its very center the same brilliant diamond. If acid and tools and skill and labor were applied, instead of the handful of black mudballs there would lie a handful of precious gems, the very same as the spotless white diamond facing them.

Thus, as every mudball was at its heart a diamond, so every individual is at its center a Christ. It was Jesus who revealed to us our real Self. It was this Christ that he saw in every man.

> I am come that they might have life, and that they might have it more abundantly ... Whosoever drinketh of the water that I shall give him, shall never thirst; but the water that I shall give him, shall be in him a well of water springing tip into ever-lasting life ... And ye shall know the truth, and the truth shall make you free ... Nothing shall be impossible to you ... Behold, the kingdom of God is within you.

Spiritual understanding demonstrates the Holy Ghost, divine Science. Understanding of spiritual Science is the line of demarcation between the real and the unreal. We need have no fear as we pass the line, or vision toward it, for here we catch the cry, "Not by might, nor by power, but by my Spirit ... For by strength shall no man prevail ... And they shall fight against thee; but they shall not prevail against thee; for I am with thee, to deliver thee."

It is the upward vision that rolls the mountains into the sea; that causes the heart to leap with joy and shout the universal freedom of life. It is above the line of demarcation that we see the flowing streams of living waters and

103

the refreshing bread from heaven—hear, see and feel the things of the finished kingdom. It is above the line of demarcation that we behold the Christ, the Messiah.

We should let nothing satisfy us but laying hold of the Highest—the universal God! The cosmic Christ! We should understand that the ideal teacher is he who tells us of the Christ, the real Self; shows us how to find this Christ; how to quicken our intuition, how to understand the mystical saying of Jesus, "I, if I be lifted up." This is a height beyond the mind.

It was with the sense of his lighted Soul that Jesus declared himself the light of the world. He went apart with his disciples:

> And Jesus told the twelve about the inner light that cannot fail; about the kingdom of the Christ within the soul; about the power of faith; about the secret of the resurrection of the dead; about immortal life ...
>
> (And Jesus said to the Jews) "Why murmur you, and reason thus among yourselves. The Christ is everlasting Life; he came from heaven; he has the keys of heaven, and no man enters into heaven except he fills himself with Christ. I came in flesh to do the will of God, and lo, this flesh and blood are filled with Christ; and so I am the living bread that comes from heaven. And when you eat this flesh and drink this blood you will have everlasting life, and, if you will, you may become the bread of Life.
>
> And many of the people were enraged ... and his disciples were aggrieved because he said these things, and many turned away and followed him no more ... They could not comprehend the parable he spoke. And Jesus said, You stumble and fall before the truth; what will you do when you shall see this flesh and blood transmuted into higher form?
>
> The flesh is naught; the Spirit is the quickening power. The words I speak are Spirit ... God feeds the soul direct from heaven; the bread of life comes from above ... If you will give your life in service of

your fellow men, then you will save your life. This life is but a span, a bauble of today. There is a life that passes not. Where is your profit if you gain the world and lose your soul? If you would find the spirit life, the life of man in God, then you must walk a narrow way and enter through a narrow gate. The way is Christ, and you must come by the way of Christ. No man comes into God but by the Christ ...

Thus, Jesus, taking Peter, James and John, went forth unto a mountain top to pray. And as he prayed, a brilliant light appeared; his form became as radiant as a precious stone; his face shone like the sun; his garments seemed as white as snow. The son of man became the Son of God. He was transfigured that the men of earth might see the possibilities of man ... and they saw the glory of the Lord; and more, they saw the glory of the heavenly world, for they beheld two men from thence stand forth beside the Lord ...

These men are Moses and Elijah, who come that you may know that heaven and earth are one ... The veil that separates the worlds is but an ether veil. For those who purify their hearts by faith the veil is rolled aside, and they can see and know that death is an illusive thing.

And Moses and Elijah talked with Jesus on the mount. They talked about the coming trial of the Lord; about his death, his rest within the tomb; about the wonders of the resurrection morn, the transmutation of his flesh, and his ascension on the clouds of light—all symbolic of the path that every man must tread; symbolic of the way the sons of men become the sons of God.

The three disciples were amazed, and suddenly the ethers were surcharged with song, and forms as light as air moved about the mountain top. And then from out of the glory of the upper world they heard a voice that said, "This is the son of man, my chosen one to manifest the Christ to men. Let all the earth hear him."

—*The Aquarian Gospel*

The Christ is never born; the Christ never died and is never resurrected. The Christ *is*! The Christ is born in you and in me as we recognize and understand the reality of Life. The individual identity of Christ is born on earth, and while there are infinite identities of the Christ represented as you and me, still there is but one Christ, as there is but one God. Christ, the impersonal Truth of God, heals the sick, stills the waters, lights the path, talks to us, walks with us, delivers us!

> And o'er earth's troubled, angry sea,
> I see Christ walk,
> And come to me, and tenderly,
> Divinely talk.
>
> —Mary Baker Eddy

When Jesus was but seven years old, he stood before the people gathered in his home and related to them a vision that he had:

> I had a dream, and in my dream, I stood before a sea, upon a sandy beach. The waves upon the sea were high; a storm was raging on the deep. Someone above gave me a wand. I took the wand and touched the sand, and every grain of sand became a living thing; the beach was all a mass of beauty and song. I touched the waters at my feet, and they were changed to trees and flowers and singing birds, and everything was praising God.
>
> I heard a voice which said, "There is no death! The sea of life rolls high; the storms are great. The multitude of men are idle, listless, waiting, like dead sand upon the beach. Your wand is truth. With this you touch the multitudes, and every man becomes a messenger of holy light and life. You touch the waves upon the sea of life; their turmoils cease; the very winds become a song of praise. There is no death, because the wand of truth can change the dryest bones to living things, bring the loveliest flowers from stagnant ponds, and turn the most discordant notes to harmony and praise.
>
> —*The Aquarian Gospel*

He who has found the Christ knows that Truth doeth all these things and that even greater things may be done, so great that it has not yet entered into our hearts to conceive them. As we let impersonal Christ be our teacher, we find:

> Much study is a weariness of the flesh ... For while one saith, "I am of Paul," and another, "I am of Apollos," are ye not carnal? ... I have planted, Apollos watered; but God gave the increase. So then neither is he that planteth anything, neither he that watereth; but God that giveth the increase ... Let no man glory in men. Ye are Christ's; and Christ is God's.

The understanding that there is but one God, impersonal and universal, and one Christ, impersonal and universal, takes away all sense of personality, personal teacher, or personal student. It is Jesus Christ that we follow and obey! It is Jesus Christ that we honor and serve! It is Jesus Christ that we love!

It is the *Christ* Science, divine Science, that teaches us the deep things of Life. It is divine Science that makes plain the Christ of God. It is divine Science that performs miracles. It is divine Science that brings heaven upon earth, unifies mankind, removes vain glory, and feels divine Love.

> There is but one way to heaven, harmony, and Christ in divine Science shows us this way ... We must learn that God is infinitely more than a person, or finite form, can contain; that God is a divine *Whole*, and *All*, an all-pervading intelligence and Love, a divine, infinite Principle ...
>
> I believe in God as the Supreme Being. I know not what the person of omnipotence and omnipresence is, or what the infinite includes ...
>
> Divine metaphysics is that which treats of the existence of God, His essence, relations, and attributes ... The Christ was Jesus' spiritual selfhood; therefore

> Christ existed prior to Jesus ... There is but one
> Christ ... Christ, as the true, spiritual idea, is the ideal
> of God now and forever, here and everywhere.
>
> —Mary Baker Eddy

Being spiritually minded, we readily discern that Christ is the real man, the hidden, inner Self, which is eternally one with God and is never born and will never die. Truth was before Jesus appeared to us, and Truth is now and ever shall be. Christ is the individual God-Self. It was this Christ that Jesus portrayed. This is the Christ who declares, "I am the Way! I am the Life! I am the Truth! I am the bread of Life! I am the Resurrection!"

Jesus of Nazareth, charged with the consciousness of his own divinity, recognized his God-power. It was this truth that the intuitive Peter grasped when he exclaimed to Jesus, "Thou art the Christ, the Son of the living God." And Jesus answered, "Blessed art thou, for flesh and blood hath not revealed it unto thee, but my Father, which is in heaven."

We speak from our Christ center, as we declare, "I am perfect! I am well! I see! I hear! I know!"

Having exalted view, we find exalted thought breaking forth for us from the limitless reservoir within. We declare, "Because I am whole, therefore am I healed! It is finished!"

Beholding the universal I AM and Its universal Christ is our heavenly bread, is our living water and spiritual quickening. We let go dark shadows of imagination and take hold of eternal Life.

"Cast your burdens upon me" is the cry of ever-present Truth. Rise up and know that you are that which cannot be sick, that which cannot be poor, that which cannot be mournful, that which cannot die. *I* am Life of your life! *I* am substance of your being! Ye are the light of the world! You could no more lose your life than the water could cease to wet or the sun could cease to shine.

I am one Presence, one Power, filling all heaven and all earth—Myself, All! Since you *are*, you are in, of, and from Myself and are pure and holy, whole and immortal—the Christ of the finished kingdom!

Far more wonderful than the discoveries of the hidden gold in the earth, the new stars in the heavens, or the hidden secrets of the ancient tombs of kings is the discovery by you, and by me, of the Christ within.

The apostles were given authority by Jesus to preach the gospel, heal the sick, cast out devils, raise the dead "in my name." So have we this same authority.

Jesus Christ is the name of the great Potentate—the name of God, the Son, the name of the finished kingdom. This is the name that is "far above all principality, and power, and might, and dominion, and every name that is named" (Eph. 1:21).

How did Peter heal the man that was born lame? "In the name of Jesus of Nazareth, rise up and walk." And later he repeated and emphasized it: "Be it known unto you all that by the name of Jesus Christ, even by him doth this man stand here before you whole." Still again, the third time did the fearless and inspirational Peter cry, "Neither is there salvation in any other; for there is none other name under heaven given among men, whereby we must be saved."

Suppose you were walking quietly in the street, paying strict attention to your own business, and along came a man who dragged you into court, proclaiming that you were mistreating him, that you struck him and knocked him down. Now, what would you do? Why, you would call upon the name of the law. You would furnish witnesses to prove that you did not even speak to him and never touched him, and the law would free you.

Now, dear people, as there is a name of the law on the lesser plane, so there is a name of the law on the highest plane, and the name of this saving power is the name *Jesus Christ*.

When we call upon the name of the law of the lesser planes, what does it mean? It means fair trial in court; the right to defend ourself and prove our innocence.

When we call upon the name of Jesus Christ, what does this mean? It means healing, deliverance. The name *Jesus Christ* stands for the man of the finished kingdom, and when we call upon this name or declare Truth "in his name," we simultaneously call for the miracle, the instantaneous deliverance which he taught, demonstrated, and promised us all.

There is no personality attached to this name. It does not mean the name of a personal man or a personal savior. It is the name of the spiritualized man, the cosmic Christ! We all bear this name. "What I have done, all men will do; and what I am, all men will be," pronounced the risen Christ—to you, to me.

What were the promises made us by this Morning Star? Listen: "And whatsoever ye shall ask in my name, that will I do ... If ye shall ask anything in my name, I will do it ... Hitherto, ye have asked nothing in my name; ask, and ye shall receive, that your joy may be full."

Remember, a name stands for something. As the name Peter stands for power, the name James stands for thought, and the name John stands for love, so the name Jesus Christ stands for the combined attributes of the I AM That I AM—all glory, all salvation, all joy, all love, all wholeness, all abundance, all perfection.

Let us pronounce ourself whole "in his name." Let us look upon the sick who come to us for help and pronounce them whole in the name of the Christ of God, the representative of the finished kingdom—the Christ that was never born, never crucified, and that never died; the always risen, the always living Christ!

"The first man Adam was made a living soul; the last Adam was made a quickening spirit." The first man, Adam, represents the man of the lesser kingdoms, while the last man, Jesus Christ, represents the heavenly man, the man who belongs to the victorious fourth dimension—who turned water into wine; who stilled the storm and multiplied the bread; who passed unseen through angry throngs; who gave feet to the lame, ears to the deaf, eyes to the blind, mind to the idiots, soul to the sinners, heart to the heartless, and life to the dead!

What greater name do we want? What greater name could we have? What greater name shall we stand for than the name *Jesus Christ*, the Son of God, who *finished* the work he came to do?

Therefore, in the name of him who finished his work, in the name of the Christ of God, let the deaf hear these words; let the blind see these words; let the unenlightened feel these words; let the lame stand up; let the sick be made whole; and let the dead arise!

> And let him that is athirst come. And whosoever will, let him take the water of life freely.
> —Rev. 22:17

111

Chapter VI

ILLUMINATION

Illumination is a state of lighted consciousness, a consciousness that is lighted from within, from above.

Intuition, inspiration, high recognition belong to the realm of the real, and they spring from illumined consciousness. Divine wisdom does not arrive through reason of the mind, but through spiritual quickening. "When the Spirit of truth is come, he will guide you into all truth" (John 16:13).

Reason, rightly used, is a gift of God. It is of great assistance in explaining and communicating truth and may serve as a necessary step toward realization. Reason without divine illumination takes one on a toilsome journey, hard and compelling. Should one make himself a servant to reason, the road becomes toilsome, dangerous. Without the inner zeal of soul, transcending and illumining the reasoning faculty, the thought is without quickening, and the tongue is without fire.

It is inspiration that hears the voice, feels the touch, sees the light. "The inspiration of the Almighty giveth them understanding" (Job 32:8). Let reason be founded on divine inspiration; then reason guides to high recognition.

Intuition and inspiration bring out the hidden treasures of the Soul-Self, disclosing the mysteries of the heavenly kingdom. Soul illumination brings starry light to the eyes, radiance to the countenance, and as one delivers the message of truth in this lighted state, his spoken words start a burning response in the hearts of his listeners.

"The children of Israel could not steadfastly behold the face of Moses for the glory of his countenance ... A man's wisdom maketh his face to shine ... And Jesus bringeth them up into an high mountain apart, and his face did shine as the sun, and his raiment was white as light."

The Absolute must be spiritually discerned. Instead of reasoning about Truth, we now *recognize* Truth. Not only do we find freedom for ourselves in so doing but we give this same freedom to others. We issue no laws or require subservience to any rules. We acknowledge no authority but the universal Executive. We feel free to read, think, act, speak as the Spirit within us directs. In this illumination and freedom, we find new law transcending that which says "Thou shalt" and "Thou shalt not."

Jesus Christ was the representative of the plane of the Absolute, the illumined kingdom. He said, "Love is the fulfilling of the law." The heavenly law is Love, which knows no thine and mine; no good and evil; no right and wrong; no cause and effect; no sin and punishment, but is above all pairs of opposites, seeing with Its own light and glory.

"Perfect love casteth out fear." Love of the perfect, the absolute, the real and true, love of the finished kingdom, illumines the heart with that Light "which lighteth every man that cometh into the world" and is our "armor of light."

Intuition, inspiration, faith, praise, command belong to the plane of the Absolute, the plane of illumined Consciousness. Many, dwelling in the mental plane to a large extent, at times unknowingly function on this supermental plane. Though mind is fastened to mental things, mental thoughts, mental laws, still its gaze is unconsciously often lifted to the realm where Reality is. The same applies to books which may be based upon right thinking yet also breathe the Spirit.

Experience of spiritual uplift comes not through a process of philosophical reasoning but springs from an awakened consciousness. One cannot attain high recognition through the avenue of reason alone. Some have obscured previous attainments and illuminations by descending and remaining in the plane of unillumined mental reasoning. It is a state of mind that may be called intoxicating for those who are satisfied to remain herein.

Let us view some definitions, as given us by Webster, that we may have an accurate conception of the accepted meaning of certain words.

Reason: Judgment; to think logically; the process of the mind, by which propositions, old or new, are reached.

Conviction: A doctrine or proposition which one firmly believes; a state of being satisfied with the mind's evidence.

Absolute: Complete; whole; perfect; the unconditioned, Self-existent Being.

Vision: A divine faculty; immediate consciousness of the real.

Faith: Recognition of spiritual realities.

Mystical: Betoking a hidden meaning. "God hath revealed a way, mystical and super natural"; nature of reality or the divine essence; the way of direct, divine illumination, by which one attains immediate consciousness of God.

Intuition: A looking upon; immediate perception of truth without conscious reasoning; mystical vision; immediate knowledge of spiritual things.

Love: The sublimest and holiest of spiritual affection, as "God is love."

Spiritual realization springs from high recognition of universal Truth and is a feeling or an experience of uplift and certainty. Mental conviction is a state of the individual mentality. This is also a feeling of certainty, but it has been reached through a process of logical reasoning and not through intuition.

Realization is a culmination reached through intuition, while mental conviction is a culmination reached through thought and reason. If mental conviction leads one to high recognition and realization, it is serving a good purpose and is blessing the individual.

Reason uses the process of analysis, while intuition is a state of illumined consciousness. Intuition is a state of knowing and feeling springing from the Soul-Self. Intuition is not founded upon reason. It can give no reason. It knows, feels, and is satisfied. Reason can always account for itself; can always find a law upon which to hinge itself or a law that hinges upon it. Intuition needs no such support. Reason searches, while divine intuition knows. The Christ-Self does not reason. The Christ-Self knows. Reason oftentimes closes the door to illumination, for reason questions, argues, discusses.

Intuition is the "still small voice," arriving at Truth without the process of labored thought or reason. Intuition belongs to the high plane, for it labors not; it is the laborless activity of "Christ in you." "I will put my law in their inward parts, and write it in their hearts" (Jer. 31:33). "It is" or "It is not" announces intuition. It takes nothing else into consideration but itself. Intuition would not be itself were it guided by reason, while reason will improve itself by listening to intuition.

Reason, thought, and feeling are wonderful gifts of universal God to each and every individual.

It is said that the bee buzzes as long as it is outside the bloom, but as soon as it settles down in the heart of the blossom, it drinks in quiet. It is similar in our thirst and effort for understanding. In proportion as we feel and understand absolute Truth, we stop labored effort. "Labor not," said the illumined Master.

Individual man is potentially a spiritual being, and his destined attainment is the manifestation of perfection. The Soul that we are is like a circle without beginning and without end; we can neither add to it nor take from it. We recognize, through illumination, its completeness and immortality.

New birth is the birth in consciousness of the illumined Christ. It is the spiritual birth, bringing new order, new life, new joy. All great teachers discern that we come into this new birth through inspiration, illumination, love.

What is called the evolution of man is his rise in consciousness from the awareness of his individual center of light to the experience of cosmic Consciousness. This illumined sense of infinity, the oneness of all, transcends the mind and lights the Self. It is a Soul experience, in which is found no evil. Evil is but a thought creation found in the planes of thoughts and things, but evil is not present in the plane of illumined Consciousness.

The Master of vision declared, "Thy kingdom come on earth, as it is in heaven." It is possible for us here and now to experience heavenly joy, illumination, and freedom. Called into the synagogues or before magistrates, shall one reason out what he shall say in his defense? No. Said the Master, "Take ye no thought how or what thing ye shall answer, or what ye shall say, for it shall be given you in that same hour what ye shall speak."

If one is in great danger, is it necessary that he stop and "declare Truth" or give a reason to himself why he will be delivered? No. "I will be with thee. I will not fail thee nor forsake thee," says the all-knowing Presence.

If one is in prison, bound hand and foot, must he "treat" or look into books or call upon himself to save himself? If he has been living in the spirit of illumination, facing the most High, looking to the great Deliverer for things mighty and strong, an angel can touch him, as Peter felt, and with his senses illumined and lighted, he can step from the shackles as though they were not. Doors can spring open of their own accord; that which is considered solid can become as vapor. Such is high salvation—the salvation of high illumination.

If one is in trouble, what shall he do? Shall he sit and think thoughts or read words; concentrate or use suggestions? He looks to the most High, the real Self, and it is given him what to think. The value of high recognition is that it uplifts the mind or lights up the mind, and naturally it comes in contact with cosmic harmony and order.

To educate the mentality so that one can reason, analyze, and arrive at right conclusion or mental conviction of Truth is one thing, but to have spiritual insight, keen awareness, faith, and illumination is another thing. The key that unlocks one realm does not unlock the other.

Jesus, the highly illumined, could have called forth ministering angels from the high plane, but he chose to give his life a ransom for us. He knew the answer to the question "What is Truth?" and he knew the answers to the mysteries of the finished kingdom. But he often spoke in heavenly language, which was not comprehended by his listeners.

The mystery of love and marriage was understood by Jesus, and when he was asked about the woman who married seven times and her future relation to the seven men in heaven, Jesus did not reply from the plane of reason;

hence, his answer is little understood. He was speaking from intuition, the plane of Spirit. His answer was: in this plane of life, men marry to gratify themselves or to perpetuate the race, but in the heavenly world, men do not take upon themselves such marriage vows.

In every plane of life, we find a new order, and in the heavenly plane, though men taketh not the marriage vows as here on earth, this does not annihilate love or marriage, but love and marriage are of higher order— the union of hearts, the union of that which God hath forever joined together!

While that which is called flesh and bones will be transmuted into an embodiment of higher order, yet we feel certain that we shall recognize and know our loved ones and enjoy the celestial glories and beauties of the new heaven and new earth. On the mount of transfiguration Jesus' face shone like the sun, and his raiment was whiter than anything the disciples had ever beheld; still, they knew it was Jesus.

"What is prayer?" ask some. Prayer is meditation, and it is more than meditation. Prayer is affirmation, and it is more than affirmation. Prayer is divine illumination, high recognition and realization of the true facts of life. Ideas change, opinions change, conceptions change, prayers change, but God is the *changeless* I AM—the unalterable Absolute.

There is a perfect, finished idea of everything in the finished kingdom. We would not recognize sickness as abnormal were it not for the true idea of health. We would not recognize death as an "enemy" were it not for the true idea of eternal life. There is but one true creation—the absolute, spiritual creation—and prayer, known as desire, meditation, declaration, or command, uplifts or lifts up the individual sense to recognize and experience Reality— cosmic Consciousness.

In the finished kingdom, the fields are already white to harvest; the future is already the now; the desire is already fulfilled. Illumination is ever-present; the kingdom is on earth as it is in heaven.

One can live without illumination, believing in the reality of evil, yet this in no way interferes with perfection itself. No death will ever stop the onward moving current of life; no mistake will ever interfere with heavenly law; no wrong viewpoint will ever change the vision of Life Itself; no thought will ever alter that which already *is*; no darkness will ever touch the illumined Absolute.

Prayer rises from the individual himself, and all answer to prayer comes from *one* source—the Highest and the Inmost are identical.

All that we are or ever will be is within us, as above us. All mysteries, wonders, and miracles, all answers to our questions lie in the depths of our being. It is by reaching upward and outward to the great Universal that the inward is quickened and illumined.

All mode of mental treatment or prayer that is not based upon perfection must be superseded by a more spiritual and more illumined insight. Buds of plants and leaves of trees need air, water, light, and warmth, that they burst open into maturity. It takes faith, love, trust, and right recognition, that the secrets of our inner Nature are disclosed to us.

Illumination shows us two ways of overcoming, or coming over and up to the standpoint of the Absolute. We find these two methods depicted in the two pictures of Daniel in the lions' den. In one picture, we see Daniel facing the lions; in the other picture, we see Daniel facing the Light.

Let us examine, with illumined attention, the first position—Daniel facing the lions. When difficulties confront us, do we feel like running away from them, or do we face them? To face them in the right way is to look above them and beyond them and, through illumination, recognize their nothingness.

A man was struggling with what seemed to him a problem of life and death. His seeming condition caused him such paroxysms of intense pain that he flung himself upon the bed and cried aloud. The thought came to him, "I must be healed now, or I will die. What shall I do? What shall I think?" He reached out for the answer. It came from within: "Thou preparest a table before me in the presence of mine enemies."

Forgetting his fear and trouble for the moment, he sat upright in his chair. What was the meaning of this verse? What did this message signify? He repeated the words: *in the presence of mine enemies.* Was he not now in the presence of the enemy—disease, pain, death? But the promise is: Thou preparest a table for me *in their presence.*

Suddenly the hidden meaning dawned upon him. Illumination came: right when the lions are facing us, divine refreshment, spiritual understanding, is *already prepared, already sufficient.*

He glanced at the clock; according to its count, in five more minutes another attack was due. He determined to live this five minutes facing the "enemy," feeling back of him and above him the "table prepared," the omnipotent Truth upholding him. Placing his hands firmly on the arms of the chair, he faced the lions—the belief of pain and death—and with illumined sense, he cried, "Come! I am unafraid of you, for what God Almighty is, is greater than what you seem to be!" Like an armored knight he waited. But the lions' mouths were closed; the enemy came not. Only the silence answered him, and the clock ticked on.

For one hour he sat still, his mind a blaze of light and power. He arose, *well*, healed of what doctors would have pronounced fatal. Gone is the darkness when light touches it. Gone are the lions when the I AM speaks Its own name!

We can also face the Light, our back to the lions. A woman was told by doctor and nurse at her bedside that she would probably die—symptoms were fatal. Dismissing everyone from her room, she called back one member and asked for a book that lay on the table. Alone with the book, she lay still for a few moments; then came the thought, "While I do live I will face the Light!"

She turned entirely away from the belief of disease and death, as though they were not present, and upward she looked, toward the Light. For several moments she thought about life, how glorious to live, how wonderful is life! She noticed not the lions—death—standing back of her. Presently she opened the book with the cry, "Give me one sentence to carry with me as I go on to Life!" The book fell open to these three words: "Life is triumphant!"

Like a flash of lightning, swift as the swiftest arrow, there shot into her being, like a living flame, the illumination: "Then I *cannot* die!" Instantly the phantom, death, vanished. She arose from her bed, whole and well.

We victoriously face the lions, *knowing their nothingness* and feeling our heavenly dominion. We lovingly face the Light, feeling Its *allness*, which knows no evil. It takes tremendous courage to face lions, feeling our greatness and their nothingness. It takes illumined faith and transcendent trust to face the Light, paying no attention to the lions that roar behind us.

God is that which is back of us! God is that which is before us! "I am the first and I am the last!"

He who illuminates his mind with recognition and contemplation of heavenly things has entered a new order. He who places the inner eye toward the finished kingdom has entered a new freedom. He who feels the oneness of all lives, the omnipresence of all love and harmony, has entered a new peace and illumination.

Ever, illumined Life calls to us:

Look unto Me! Love Me! Praise Me! Glorify Me! Command Me! Nothing shall be impossible to you, for My omnipotence is your omnipotence. My illumination is your illumination!

Why stay in the valley, when heights are calling us? Why stay in darkness when the Light is overshining us? Why labor with thought and things while angels stand ready to deliver us? Looking away from graves and tombstones, away from the "end of the world," away from strife and war, away from evil, we see as God sees—we judge as God judges. What is the judgment of the I AM?

And God saw everything that he had made, and behold, it was very good!

That which was, is, and that which is, hath already been. Come ye blessed! Look above things, above thoughts; above the faces of angels, friends, powers, forces. Disciples of Truth, consider these good and right and true manifestations of My Love and My Omnipotence, but let not thy gaze rest here as salvation. Look to Me, the Giver of gifts, the Origin of intelligence, the Absolute Self-existent *First*!

Let us be up and doing! Let us keep our minds quickened and illumined with divine inspiration, remembering that Spirit is the real and eternal!

One may be able, with individual power of individual mind, to do great things, but the way that leads to eternal salvation is not one of laborious action. It is a narrow way, lying among rocks and pitfalls; yet in the path itself is no pitfall. In this path, we hear the words "Labor not! Take no thought! In such an hour as ye think not!"

The recognition of the finished kingdom proceeds from inner illumination. The king of the heavenly kingdom is Love. It is through divine Love that we recognize, realize, and manifest the wonders which are already prepared for us.

"For since the beginning of the world men have not heard, nor perceived by the ear, neither hath the eye seen … what he hath prepared for him that waiteth for him" (Isa. 64:4).

Come, inherit the kingdom prepared
for you from the foundation of the world!

Chapter VII

FAITH

Faith is the door that opens into the finished kingdom. Faith is the quality of mind that believes in the announcement "There hath not failed one word of all his good promise" (1 Kings 8:56).

"Except ye become as little children, ye shall not enter into the kingdom of heaven," declared the great Jesus. Faith is a simple, trusting state of mind, without question or doubt. Faith arrives at conclusions intuitively. It visions toward the finished kingdom with illumined, inner urge. It beholds the invisible as though it were visibly present. It understands that Truth *is* and that we *already have.*

Faith in the universal I AM, faith in the universal Christ, faith in the oneness and unity of God the Father and God the Son, faith in the ever-manifested harmony and glory of the finished kingdom is ideal faith—the faith of God.

It is faith that sees the white Christ where the sinner seems to stand. It is faith that beholds the perfect man where the sick one apparently is. It is faith that, looking up, calls to the man in the sepulchre, "Come forth!"

Though faith uses not two outer eyes with which to vision, it is not blind. "Thou canst not behold me with thy two outer eyes; I have given thee an eye divine." The eye that beholds the supernal Presence and beholds the finished kingdom is the incorporeal eye.

"Unto thee lift I up mine eyes, O thou that dwellest in the heavens (heavenly kingdom) … Lift up your eyes (incorporeal vision) and look on the fields; for they are white already to harvest ... Lift up thine eyes unto the high places! ... The hearing ear, and the seeing eye, the Lord hath made even both of them ... The light of the body is the eye (spiritual vision): if therefore thine eye be single (looking toward the finished kingdom), thy body shall be full of light (wholeness) ..."

"Eyes (outer or uninspired vision) have they, but they see not (invisible things) ... Blessed are your eyes, for they see; and your ears, for they hear ... Let thine eyes be open, and let thine ears be attentive ... And when ye see this, your heart shall rejoice ..."

"And Jesus lifted up his eyes on his disciples and said, Blessed are ye that hunger now (for heavenly food): for ye shall be filled ... And Jesus lifted up his eyes, and said, Father, I thank thee that thou hast heard me ... Lazarus, come forth! ... Then Jesus took the five loaves and two fishes, and looking up to heaven, he blessed them, and brake, and gave to the disciples to set before the multitude ... Jesus lifted up his eyes to heaven, and said, 'Father, the hour is come; glorify thy Son, that thy Son may also glorify thee."

It is as we look up to the finished kingdom with spiritual vision, the eye of faith, love, and high recognition, that we behold heavenly things prepared for us and shout with John, "That which was from the beginning, which we have heard, which we have seen with our eyes, which we have looked upon ... declare we."

"At that day shall a man look to his Maker ... Look unto the rock whence ye are hewn. Look, ye blind, that ye may see" (Isaiah).

"We, according to his promise, look for new heavens and a new earth, wherein dwelleth righteousness ... Unto them that look for him shall he appear the second time, without sin unto salvation … And I saw a new heaven and a new earth … Behold, the tabernacle of God is with men, and he will dwell with them; and they shall be his people, and God himself shall be with them, and be their God."

We cannot behold the heavenly kingdom, looking back of us. "No man … looking back, is fit for the kingdom of God" (Luke 9:62). We lift our eyes to the hills. We give attention to high Truth. We are of high watch! We have the faith of God! Nothing but immersion in the chemical waters of faith rouses Soul-quickening. Blessed are they who drink at the fountain of transcendental faith!

Let us harmonize our mind with heavenly facts of Life: From Light, all light comes; from Life, all life comes; from the Fountainhead, all individual consciousness comes. Discovering that good which has been since the beginning of the world, we experience joy and peace. This is the cosmic vision of cosmic Life—the *finished kingdom*!

We base our thinking and reasoning on the already perfect, and with illumined faith we behold ourself free Spirit—unconditioned, unfettered, all powerful, all victorious. One can build temples to the skies, attain wealth, fame, name, and apparent happiness, but except he recognize himself *above* his thought, *above* his body, *above* all conditions, he has not achieved high recognition, illumined faith, incorporeal vision.

The creative Life that brought us here is that Life that lives in us, as us; that works in us, delivers us. We recognize this Life and our life as one, for as the wave is a state of the ocean, so the consciousness that we are is a state of the creative Life Itself. It was the recognition of this high Truth that prompted Jesus to inquire: Why do you toil? Why have you so little faith in the great Infinite? Why do you not consider the lily, how it grows and how wondrously it is arrayed in spotless white? Why do you not learn a lesson from the flowers in the fields or the birds in the air?"

And the same Christ asks today: Why do you toil so much with thoughts and reasons? Why do you labor with thought until your head aches and your heart despairs? Be still, look up, and have faith as the smallest seed that grows. All is already created! All is forever finished! Think in harmony with universal Truth! Vision in harmony with universal Vision! Have the faith that Life forever has in Itself!

In order that we feel exaltation and tranquility, we place our feet firmly in the narrow way and in all earnestness and sincerity extend helping, loving hands to those seeking our support. We feel the nearness, the allness of God, and we have faith and joy that "it is finished." Paul, recognizing this truth of the finished creation, declared:

> As we have borne the image of the earthy, we shall also bear the image of the heavenly. For we know that if our earthy house were dissolved, we have a building of God, a house not made with hands, eternal in the heavens.

The heavenly body is the transcendental body, the spiritual body, the body of the finished kingdom. "And it came to pass, while he blessed them, he was parted from them, and carried up to heaven (the heavenly plane): While they beheld, he was taken up; and a cloud received him out of their sight."

"The fruit of the Spirit is love, joy, peace ... faith. Till we all come in the unity of the faith, and of the knowledge of the Son of God, unto a perfect man ... Above all, taking the shield of faith ... Without faith it is impossible to please God ... Let him ask in faith, nothing wavering."

Jesus' life on earth was one thrilling example of faith. No wonder the disciples, discovering this, cried to him, "Increase our faith." Jesus was quick to recognize faith in the hearts that approached him for help. "And Jesus said, How is it ye have no faith? ... Have faith in God ... When the Son of man cometh, shall he find faith on the earth? ... Daughter, be of good comfort; thy faith hath made thee whole; go in peace! ... Receive thy sight: thy faith hath saved thee! ... Arise. Go thy way; thy faith hath made thee whole!"

If one finds it difficult to illumine his vision, to quicken his spirit, let him bring forth more faith. Let him go off to the hills or by the rippling brookside or into the fields of flowers and birds and get in vital touch with universal Life Itself. How can one feel God as within him except he recognize God as without him? Beholding universal Omnipresence and the manifested wonders and glories of Nature inspires the heart, quickens the Spirit, and touches the chord that thrills with the harmony of the Universe.

Have we not all had moments when we felt the peace that passeth telling and understanding; when we were without conscious thought of any kind; when our mind was placid, like a crystal lake; when our body was without sensation, still; when light seemed within us and without us; when all limitations were gone; when all reason had fled; when we were illuminated and the illumined one?

Many ask, "How can I waken divine faith and Soul illumination in another?" One can teach another, help another, bless another, but no one can have faith for another. No one can find God universal or God individual for another. Each must do his own finding and experiencing. No one can drink water for us or eat food for us. No one can experience faith and quickening for us. To look up and reach up with inner attention to perfect God and perfect creation is the first step in the spiritual awakening of the individual.

Faith is not a quality of the intellect. Faith is a state of consciousness. Faith is "enduring as seeing the invisible." Faith beholds substantial things, unseen. Faith is the revivifying fountain of Soul elixir. It brings warmth and feeling that is followed by courage, power, and command. What is command without high faith? What is courage without high faith? What is glory without high faith? What is success without high faith? "Except the Lord build the house, they labor in vain that build it (Ps. 127:1)

Faith and love may seem too simple for the complicated mind, yet we can make no lasting attainment without them. When our thought is on fire with faith, love, and divine illumination, the ever-present Christ stands forth within us. Sublime faith hurls the mountain into the sea and rends the darkness with transcendent light. Let us inbreathe faith. Let us breathe out faith.

Faith takes away fear. Let him who is fearful attain to faith. True courage cannot be present without faith upon which to stand. Working mentally for courage and strength may bring momentary response, but in order to have lasting and permanent courage, we must have right faith. When faith is present, one need not work mentally for courage; he *is* courage. When one strives for fearlessness in a mental way, he is not building his house upon the rock; he is not looking toward the finished kingdom, which immediately causes faith to rise up in him. Faith in the finished kingdom simultaneously brings courage.

Many, placing God as without themselves, ignorant of God as also within themselves, have attained to great success, great triumphs, great achievements, for unconsciously looking to God universal wakens God individual, and in due season the individual perceives that there is a without, universal God, and there is a within, individual Christ of God—God the Father and God the Son—and the Father and the Son are *one*.

Many, placing faith in the God within, ignorant of God without, the Fountainhead—the power that their power is, the courage that their courage is, the life that their life is, the faith that their faith is—fail to demonstrate because the recognition of the inner Christ of God does not *include* the universal Origin, the Beginning, the Source of that which one is. Hence, this state of mind is a shutting-off position. To shut oneself off from the Fountain of one's individual life is folly; nay, more—it is dangerous and fatal to progress. The limb cannot cut itself from the trunk, declaring, "I am the tree; I have life in myself," and live. It cannot remain alive, cut from the source of its life. "He that hath ears to hear, let him hear."

They who have not discovered that the Highest and the Inmost is one have not reached high recognition. Faith in ever-present Life as all-living; faith in omnipotent, universal right as changeless, victorious and triumphant; faith in the finished kingdom of wholeness and abundance; faith in God the Father, faith in God the Son, faith in God the finished kingdom is *high faith*!

"Behold, I stand at the door and knock … Lift up your heads, O ye gates; and be ye lifted up, ye everlasting doors; and the King of glory shall come in. Who is this King of glory? The Lord of hosts, he is the King of glory … Alleluia; Salvation, and glory, and honor, and power unto the Lord our God."

We are all familiar with the many healings recorded in the Bible as the result of faith. "And what shall I say more, for time would fail me to tell of Gideon and of Barak and of Samson and of Jephthae; of David also, and

of Samuel, and of the prophets. Who through faith sub-
dued kingdoms, stopped the mouths of lions, quenched
the violence of fire, escaped the edge of the sword, out of
weakness were made strong, waxed valiant in fight, turned
to fight the armies of the aliens."

The harder any condition seems to be the more certain should be our faith. It is possible for us to have the
faith of God, wherein all right things are brought to pass.

The word *believe* is often misunderstood. It is a word
little used in the mental plane but a word frequently
using it very often. It means very much the same as faith—
to be firm or to be constant.

Even at the tomb of Lazarus, we hear Jesus saying
to Martha, "Said I not unto thee, that, if thou wouldest
believe, thou shouldest see the glory of God?"

"All things are possible to him who believeth. Blessed
are they that have not seen and yet have believed." It
was to Thomas that Jesus addressed these words. Thomas
wanted to behold with his two outer eyes. He reasoned
that if he saw the prints of the nails, this would be a
visible proof to him that the body was that of Jesus. His
vision was to the body of Jesus. Jesus, recognizing the
incredulity of Thomas, lovingly rebuked him, pointing
to illumined faith: "Blessed are they who have not seen,
and yet have believed."

High faith believes without outward or visible proof.
Blessed are they of faith, they who believe, said the
Christ.

> O for a faith that will not shrink
> Though pressed by every foe;
> That will not tremble on the brink
> Of any earthly woe.
>
> A faith that shines more bright and clear
> When tempests rage without;

> That, when in danger, knows no fear,
> In darkness feels no doubt.
>
> Lord, give us such a faith as this,
> And then, what e'er may come,
> We taste e'en here the hallowed bliss
> Of an eternal home!
>
> —W.H. Bathurst

They who are struggling and fighting, they who are bearing heavy burdens—come, into this higher sense of illumined faith and universal freedom!

An earnest and faithful worker in Truth had not received his healing of what is called a rupture, which had been in appearance for several years. He had worked earnestly in Science, but the healing had not arrived. One summer's day, he was at work in the hayfield, but his suffering was so great because of the strenuous labor that he was performing that he was forced to seek the house for rest.

Presently the thought came to him, "You may never be healed of this trouble; you should consider some surgical help or an operation." But this man, being strong in the Spirit and of superb faith in spiritual healing, sprang upon his feet and from his Christ-view cried aloud, "No, I will die first!"

Seizing his hat, off again he went to the hayfield, finishing the work with no further murmur from his body. The next day, when he chanced to think of himself, he found the rupture gone.

"Act as though *I* were, and thou shalt know *I am!*"

A woman held her little boy in her arms the greater part of the night because of so-called measles making their appearance. In the morning, the little fellow came downstairs, his hands and face manifesting red blotches. Having finished his breakfast, he went to the hat rack, taking down his hat and coat, preparatory to a visit out of doors. It was a midwinter day. Snow lay deep upon the ground. The mother stood still, watching her boy in silence. She was facing the ordeal: "Choose ye."

Had she not prayed all night, reaching the high recognition that God's, presence fills the universe? That heavenly wholeness is *here* and *now*? That there are no measles in the *finished* kingdom? Yes, she had. Yet here was her boy, with apparent evidence contrary to her high vision, preparing to go out and play in the snow. The mother made her choice. The child passed out into the open air and, plunging headlong into a snowbank, shouted with glee.

She had chosen well. She had scaled a height. The child continued playing alone in his yard, not entering the house until several hours later; then his face was spotless, unblemished.

This same mother and this same child later met, fought, and won another battle. The mother was busy in the house when the door opened, and in came her eldest son, carrying in his arms this smaller brother, with a broken arm. An ice truck had passed over it. The mother let her boys sit down in the room, while quickly she went into the adjoining room to be alone. "I did not treat," she said. "I couldn't. The thing that I must know was this: did I have faith enough to believe that the bone could be set without the help of a surgeon? Did I have faith enough?' This was the paramount question with me. Then I reached out and up, and cried, "O God, give me faith enough!" At this moment, the older boy called, "Mother, come quick!" And when she entered the room: "Mother, the bones went together just now. We both heard them snap into place."

"Before they call, I will answer, and while they are yet speaking, I will hear." Behold, *I* am a God at hand.

Such is heavenly law ever acting for those who have transcendental faith. Many of us do not now experience such wonderful things; many of us do not bring forth such marvelous faith; many of us would fall in such a testing time. But some have stood the test. Some have reaped the victory. Let this spur us on to greater endeavor, greater faith, greater accomplishment.

"That which is eternal in Being is also eternal in manifestation. The thing that is eternally being manifested, remains eternally manifested" (A.K. Mozumdar).

To know that Truth *is*, to know that the manifestation of Truth *is*—this is heavenly vision and heavenly faith. We are walking in a finished kingdom; finished in plan, order, and manifestation. Not only should we think this truth but we should *feel* this truth. Peter felt this illumining faith and quickening when, with one sermon, he converted three thousand people. Paul felt this quickening, for, perceiving the faith of the crippled man, he said, "Stand upright on thy feet!" We recognize the superb faith of Jesus, the great faithful, when he cried, "Father, I thank thee that thou hast heard me." Then he called to the sleeping Lazarus, "Come forth!"

Sublime faith is ever followed by kingship, heavenly authority that says to the sick man, "Stand forth!" and to the erring claim, "Come out of him!"—that stills the storm and walks over the waves. Faith leadeth into kingship.

> "Kings exercise lordship," said Jesus. How shall one be king except his kingship be roused? ... "By me kings reign," saith the Great Voice that John turned to see. If lions do not stand back, warrings do not cease, and diseases do not retire, the true kingship is not among us ...
> Then the disciples asked him to increase their faith. But he answered them nothing. For faith, which is kingship exercising to call the God of Lazarus to

come forth and the God of the withered arm to appear, is the deepest secret of all the deep secrets of the *Magia Jesu Christi* ...

Speak boldly, looking into the face of the answering Substance, "Deliver Thou me from evil! Give me this day, my super-substantial bread! Give me courage, confidence to insist! Bless me with life, wisdom, divine efficiency!"

—E. C. Hopkins

Our God is transcendent! John, the disciple of love, beheld with lighted vision the heavenly order, the real heaven and the real earth. He saw and heard with incorporeal senses, senses that are wholly divine and spiritual. He beheld the city, New Jerusalem—the finished kingdom that is here and now. He says, "I looked, and I beheld."

We must first turn our gaze in the right direction, and then walk that way ... fixing your gaze on the realities supernal, you will rise to the spiritual consciousness of being, even as the bird which has burst from the egg and preens its wings for a skyward flight ... Turn his gaze from the false evidence of the senses to the harmonious facts of Soul and immortal being ... Hold thy gaze to the light, and the iris of faith, more beautiful than the rainbow ... will span thy heavens of thought.

We must look where we would walk ... We must look deep into realism ... The disciple looks toward the imperishable things of Spirit ... Like Elijah, look up and behold. "Look unto me and be ye saved, all the ends of the earth."

The Revelator beheld the spiritual idea from the mount of vision ... His vision is the acme of this Science ... Our own vision must be clear to open the eyes of others ... Spiritual vision is not subordinate to geometric altitudes.

These clearer, higher views inspire the Godlike man to reach the center and circumference of his being ... As mortals gain more correct views of God and man, multitudinous objects of creation, which before were invisible, will become visible ...

We must resolve to take the cross, and go forth with honest hearts to work and watch for wisdom, Truth and love ... Let us watch, work, and pray.

> Watch! till the storms are o'er,
> The cold blasts done,
> The reign of heaven begun,
> And love, the evermore.

If Spirit or the power of divine Love bear witness to the truth, this is the ultimatum, the scientific way; and the healing is instantaneous ...

Jesus beheld in Science the perfect man, who appeared to him, where sinning, mortal man appears to mortals. In this perfect man, the Saviour saw God's own likeness, and this correct view of man healed the sick!"

—Mary Baker Eddy

Our attention is now focused to God, the Father—the Source of all power, the Source of all life, the Source of all harmony. Our attention is focused to God, the Son—the Christ-Self, the Self that is above thought, above lack, above condition; the Self that is changeless, glorious, free, and eternal. Our attention is focused to God, the Holy Ghost—the finished kingdom, the manifest glory, harmony, and wholeness. *This is high Truth!*

A thought of health is a high thought, but it is not the great High. Instead of focusing our attention toward health and healing statements, we look to the Maker, the Author, the Beginning, the Sustainer of health. *This is high Truth!*

Our work, as a healer, is not to cause sickness to disappear or supply to manifest or happiness to take the place of unhappiness. Our work is to bring forth the victorious Christ—the Soul-Self. *This is high Truth!*

Right reason is healing, helpful, desirable, yet there is something back of reason and beyond reason. There is that which makes right reason possible! There is that which holds the glowing stars in the heavens; that which tints the sky with beauty and glory; that which starts the day and brings the hush of silence over all the earth at night; that which fills the depths of the earth with gold and precious gems; that which causes the lily to grow without toil or labor; that which fashioned my members "when as yet there was none of them" (Ps. 139:16).

We place our attention here to the Beginning—to that which is the cause of reason, to that which is the cause of health, to that which is the cause of beauty, to that which is the cause of abundance, to that which is the cause of ourself—the I AM THAT I AM! *This is high Truth!*

The law of mental cause and effect is swift-acting, certain, sure to those visioning toward it. We place not our attention here. We give attention to One who says, "For my thoughts are not your thoughts, neither are your ways my ways. As the heavens are higher than the earth, so are my ways higher than your ways and my thoughts than your thoughts ... I create new heavens and a new earth ... I will extend peace like a river ... and glory like a flowing stream!" *This is high Truth!*

Pressing forward to high achievements with glance upward and inward, with feet sure and certain, every link of our journey is heavenward, leading us upward in the ocean of being. We hear the Song of the Redeemed:

> And this I beheld, and, lo, a great multitude, which no man could number, of all nations, and kindreds, and people, and tongues, stood before the throne, and before the Lamb, clothed with white robes ... What are these which are arrayed in white robes? ... These

137

are they which came out of great tribulation, and have washed their robes, and made them white.

Oh, let us ever keep our vision up, up to the Highest! Let us look up, gaze up, lift up our eyes—our inner vision— to peerless Truth! Let us be still, listen, watch, and behold!

To him that overcometh will I give to eat of the hidden manna, and will give him a white stone, and in the stone a new name written, which no man knoweth, saving he that receiveth it.

Thus, new order, new hope, new joy, new inspiration, new glory forever awaits "him who overcometh," or cometh over and up to the finished kingdom.

No longer look we into the empty sepulchre, wondering where our Lord is hidden! We recognize the risen Christ before us, and we sing the Song of Moses and the Lamb!

We behold the countenance of the most High. We behold the universal Christ-Self of God. We behold the finished kingdom!

Be Thou, O God, exalted High,
And as Thy glory fills the sky,
So let it be on earth displayed,
Till Thou art here, as there, obeyed!

ABOUT THE AUTHOR

Lillian DeWaters was born in 1883 and lived in Stamford, Connecticut. She grew up with a Christian Science Background and in her early teens began to study metaphysics and on that same day to seriously study the Bible. "It was from the Bible that I learned to turn from all else to God direct .... What stood out to me above all else was the fact presented, that when they turned to God they received Light and Revelation; they walked and talked with God; and they found peace and freedom."

She published three books while actively within the Christian Science organization, and then in 1924 she had an awakening experience when it was as though a veil was parted and Truth was revealed to her. From that point she began to receive numerous unfoldments which led to her separation from the Christian Science organization.

She created her own publishing company and became a prolific writer with over 30 books published in 15 languages. She was a well-known teacher who taught regularly at the Waldorf Astoria in New York, and she was sought after as a healer throughout the world.

All of her books were written based on direct unfoldments of Absolute Truth, and each book reveals specific Truth that serious students will immediately recognize and treasure.